# LIFE STORIES
## FROM RENO TO THE AZORES

CAMILLA WALL LEE

# Publisher's Information

EBookBakery Books

Author contact: camillalee66@gmail.com

ISBN 978-1-938517-91-4

© 2019 by Camilla Wall Lee
Cover design by Holley Flagg
Cover photo by John Lee

# DEDICATION

*This book is dedicated to my family:*
*Chris and Sarah Lee, John and Jen Lee,*
*to my grandchildren Henry, Phoebe, Sam, Charlie,*
*and to the memory of my husband Charlie*

To Glennie + Norman,
Two of my favorite
people.
Camilla

# ACKNOWLEDGMENTS

A huge thank you to the members of South County Writers Group, to those who came and went, and those who solidly stayed. Without the pressure of, "It's your turn to submit," I wouldn't have written a word. And a big thank you to my editor Tracy Hart who believed in me and prodded me to continue with the pieces I wanted to shred. Thank you to my graphic designer and sister Holley Flagg for the cover design and maps. And I'm grateful to Betty Cotter for her guidance and for proofing this work with the sharp eyes of a newspaper editor. Thanks, too, to my son John Lee, for his photograph of the Narragansett coastline. And finally, thank you Michael Grossman, a solid SCWG member, for his honest critiques, and for publishing this work through his professional "eBook Bakery."

# Contents

# PROLOGUE

When going through a carton marked "writing," I'm surprised at the number of personal essays inside, each one placed in a manila folder. They were written for no one in particular other than my writing group. As each is a "stand alone" memoir piece, I'd put them away and forgotten about them. But here they are.

Spreading them out chronologically on the floor, I realize I have a timeline of my life in front of me, starting in 1950 when I was seven. The years chronicled begin with the appearance of television and end with cell phones and iPads. I re-read the recollections I'd put on paper and am inspired to publish a collection of stories for family and friends. There is a history here, not mine alone, but also of world events. I begin to edit, revise, compile, and create a legacy for the next generation. My memory for details has always been good. Perhaps not always accurate, but the pictures in my mind of events in these essays feel very clear.

The fifty years of photographs I have in crumbling albums do capture the years, but the pictures have faded. The crisp digital images buried in my computer might never be discovered after I'm gone. But unlike photographs, the written word survives.

*Camilla Lee, May, 2019*

# PREFACE

Fairly quickly into an essay by Camilla Lee, the reader knows she is in good hands. There is an immediate situation, the faintest suggestion of tension, and an intimate, almost familiar narrator. This is a woman who has had a wide breadth of experiences – living in Hong Kong and Tokyo, traveling in Europe and the East, navigating the cultural intersection of a 20th-century WASP upbringing meeting the swinging sixties. More important, she can tell us about it in a voice that is sharply observant, drily humorous, and at the same time empathetic and vulnerable.

I first met Camilla when she joined the South County Writers Group in Kingston, R.I., in 2003. I was immediately impressed by her writing, some of which was published in the newspaper I edited at the time. I should not have been surprised to learn she won a national writing award from *Redbook* magazine. With typical modesty, she usually prefaces any hand-off of a manuscript with the suggestion that it needs work, probably isn't up to snuff, etc., and she is always wrong. It proves to be polished and enthralling.

The reader of this collection has many surprises in store. Each essay captures a narrow moment in time that could only be told well by someone of Camilla Lee's talents. Enjoy, then, these freeze-frames from other worlds, near and far.

*Betty J. Cotter, March, 2019*

Betty J. Cotter, author, *Roberta's Woods, The Winters,* teacher, editor, and book reviewer

*My mother, Frederica Wall, c. 1945.*

# 1

## RENO 1950

IN 1950 I LIVED in Manhattan, had a television set and roller skates that clamped on to my brown oxfords, and went to a private girls' school. My Chapin School uniform was a light green jumper with a white blouse. All the girls in my second grade class were pretty.

That summer, between second and third grade, my mother went to Reno to get a divorce. She lived there for six weeks, long enough to become a legal resident of Nevada. In New York State, as well as other states, the rules were strict and getting a divorce could take months. But in Nevada the process was quick. The divorce rush to Reno in the 1950's was something like the Gold Rush to California one century earlier. Dude ranches flourished, serving as homes for the soon-to-be divorcées. Once the six weeks were up, you would hire a lawyer, sign papers at the courthouse, and become single again. In Nevada, the divorce trade was thriving.

My mother stayed at the Flying M.E. Ranch that seemed much like a sorority house. You could have a roommate if you needed to save money or just wanted a friend. She rode horses. At least, there's a black and white photograph of her leaning against the fence of a corral, facing the camera. She's wearing a straw cowboy hat and a denim jacket. A dark horse with a white patch stands behind her, seeming to pose as well.

On June 21st of 1950, I turned seven. For my birthday, I celebrated with a friend (my older sister Holley had already gone to Glens Falls in upstate New York to stay with cousins her age). Tina, whose parents were also divorced, was my only friend whose family hadn't left for summer vacation. Mother took us to Schraffts on 79th Street for lunch and then to a movie. The weather was oppressively hot, and a big sign: "Air Conditioned Theater," hung from the canopy of the movie house, something new at the

1

time. The next day my mother flew to Reno while I moved in with my father for a couple of nights – until he took me to Grand Central Station for the train to Camp Runoia in Belgrade Lakes, Maine.

It wasn't as though it was a surprise that I was going away to camp. I had, after all, packed my trunk with my mother. We had fun shopping at B. Altman's and carefully checked off the required items on the camp list (six pairs of cotton socks, 1 rain poncho, etc. I could only bring Ivory soap because it floats and we bathed in the lake). It wasn't until the man from Railway Express came to take away my trunk that I had begun to feel uneasy.

Grand Central terminal on that steamy day was airless, the New York heat and humidity stagnant. The huge main concourse was filled with clusters of children heading for girls' and boys' camps, with each one's name marked on a placard: Cheowonki, Brown Ledge, Teelawooket, Kieve. Going away for the summer for the first time suddenly became real when my father kissed me goodbye, and a stab of panic hit me as he left.

I took an overnight train, staying in a sleeping car full of Runoia campers. I didn't know anyone. Some of the girls in my car were already friends from the summer before – they laughed and carried on until all hours of the night. They sang camp songs. At least I felt safe in my cocoon-like berth with its curtain drawn shut. A camp staff member came by now and then to make sure I was comfortable.

After a few raw, homesick nights, when I muffled my crying under the scratchy, gray, army blanket, I pretty much glided through the rest of the summer at Camp Runoia, liking it and making friends. The screened-in cabin that was my home had eight cots, four to a side. I loved the piney smell of the moist woods, the crickets in the evening, and the birds at dawn. This was way different from the city. I loved swimming in the fresh water lake, so different from the salty ocean I was used to. We even shampooed our hair in the lake.

I was not keen on tennis and archery, but was pretty happy making lanyards out of gimp or weaving potholders inside the airy arts and crafts cabin. Once, when I had a cold, I spent the night in the infirmary, which I found extremely pleasant. The tray-table over my bed and scrambled eggs for breakfast seemed like a little holiday. I liked lying in a bed with clean sheets and listening to nature outside the window. The young nurse was attentive and pretty.

When camp was over, I was not enrolled in Chapin. My mother had come back from Reno, unmarried, and while at the Flying M.E. Ranch, she had fallen in love with a cowboy named Frank. This I knew from hearing her talk to her friend on the telephone. My father got married again (to the woman who was the cause of all this divorce business), and suddenly I had a stepmother, which bewildered me. But my manners were good, as they always were with grownups, and she was very nice.

Mother made a decision to move out west permanently. That September, she sublet our apartment on 72$^{nd}$ Street, bought a second-hand Ford, and loaded it up with suitcases of clothes and my sister and me. I brought my turtle who sloshed around in a plastic bowl with a palm tree in the center of it. The turtle stayed on the ledge inside the back window of the car. Not being the most experienced driver, my mother also got someone to share the driving duties as we made our way across the United States to Reno. Her name was Foxy. A middle-aged woman who looked down and out, she was always smoking. I recall watching the live, red ashes from her cigarettes fall down the front of her coat.

That's all I remember about Foxy, the smoking and dropping her off somewhere at a bus station. And later on, my mother saying she was crazy. She only lasted half a day.

The trip took about a week. There were no highways, just roads with route numbers, traffic lights, diners, motels, and single lanes. My assignment was to look for motels with the "AAA" symbol on an oval sign. "AAA" meant the room would be clean and the motel reputable. We drove through Salt Lake City, Utah, where I was disappointed not to find a lake filled with salt. Mostly I just looked out the car window, observing towns and houses and farms as we passed them by. From the opposite side of the car, Holley and I played a game of who could count the most cows. Together we'd decide where to eat and which diners looked like the food might not be terrible. We traveled through Wyoming, where I got an Indian doll with a removable papoose. That's where my turtle died, most likely of dehydration from the sun beating through the window.

The city of Reno had a neon sign stretching across the Truckee River saying, "The Biggest Little City in the World." The lore was that newly divorced women would throw their wedding rings over the bridge into the turbulent water below. But I don't think my mother did that. The sign is still there, standing as an historic landmark.

When we arrived, my mother found a furnished, two-bedroom apartment to rent in a square brick building. There were two apartments, one upstairs, and the one down, which was ours. The room I shared with my sister had the most disgusting dark maroon bedspreads made of a satiny material, with matching satiny curtains and dark orchid lampshades. Only a little sunlight came through the space between the draperies. It was that lush Hollywood decor of the 50's. Our landlady must have had aspirations of becoming an actress: glossy photographs dotted the walls of her in glamorous movie-star poses. There also were pictures of real movie stars: Ida Lupino, Clark Gable, and Ava Gardner.

In the hallway there was a small arched niche, designed specifically to hold a telephone. I was enchanted by this alcove and used it as a special stage for my new turtle. By now it was October. I was enrolled, a month late, for third grade at the Washoe County Elementary School – a large and colorless, rectangular cement structure. Holley went to Middle School across the street, but in the mornings, we walked together. If I was late, which happened when my mother fell behind getting organized, I would have to pick up a "tardy" slip at the principal's office. A peculiar word, "tardy." Even now when I hear it (which isn't often), it conjures up an image of handing my homeroom teacher the "tardy" slip in front of a class filled with rows of children staring at me, the new girl, with curiosity.

The school was a four-block walk from our apartment. The route wasn't a straight line; it had a couple of right-angled turns, and I often got lost on my way home. Sometimes I would get *really* lost, but I'd memorized my address and could ask for help from mothers on the sidewalk while my voice trembled and my eyes welled up.

Mother found a job working in an office downtown. The real idea behind the move was to meet up with this Frank person, the wrangler who had captured her heart. But, by the time we arrived, Frank was no longer there. He had moved on to another ranch.

Here was my mother, age 33, on her own, and clueless about survival. She had not gone to college, which at that time was not unusual. Her life consisted of being a post-debutante. My mother's career, in fact, had been serving on committees with other young wives to plan benefit fashion shows and charity balls. I have her frayed scrapbook, filled with crumbling, yellowed clippings from the society pages of the *Herald Tribune* and other papers, enjoying lunch at the Stork Club or Plaza Hotel with one co-chairwoman or another. She wore small black hats, tilted at angles. In one picture, mother is modeling a leopard-skin coat – the highlight of a fashion show by a prominent furrier. Any notion of having to support herself while trying to live on a limited sum of alimony was certainly nowhere in her imagination. She barely knew how to drive, so it was remarkable that she had driven across the country, making a desperate attempt to re-invent her life.

My mother and father had met one summer in Narragansett, Rhode Island, where mother's family had a big, shingled summer house. My father was a junior at Princeton. They fell madly in love, as twenty-year-olds do, and got married a week after his graduation from college. After the wedding, they moved from apartment to apartment in New York. Life was getting serious. My mother's picture no longer appeared in the society pages. One daughter was born and then another. Rent had to be paid. While my mother spent the summer with Holley and me in Narragansett, my father cavorted with other summer bachelors in New York City. In those days, some men acted like infidelity was acceptable.

I never did get used to my new school. I only had one friend, named Francie. She had brown, tangled hair that never seemed to be brushed and a sallow face. In the daytime, Francie's father was a card dealer at Harold's Club, a gambling casino in downtown Reno. Her mother worked there at night. Sometimes I'd go to Francie's apartment after school to play. Her mother would sleepily call out from a darkened bedroom, "Is that you, Francie?" Then she'd appear through the doorway in a chenille bathrobe and get us milk and cookies.

As for the television, which I mentioned earlier, it was a new sensation in New York but hadn't yet come to Reno. On account of the Sierra Mountain Range, it wasn't possible for Nevada to receive airwave signals from any tower. Francie had no idea what I was talking about when I tried to explain a box with a screen that you could watch movie-type things on. Reno was seeming more and more backward to me.

Francie did have a pair of roller skates, and we skated up and down her sidewalk, passing featureless two – and three-story apartment buildings. It was so unlike New York, with its buses and traffic noise and doormen whistling for taxis. But I was grateful to have Francie as we skated around the block and back again.

One nice thing about this elementary school was that I got very good grades. At my old school, I was a pretty average student and had only so-so report cards. At the Washoe County Elementary School, I was a star. The class seemed huge. A boy named Walter sat at the desk in front of me and spent most of the day with his head swiveled backward, like an owl's, studying me with interest. If I said something friendly or polite, he would turn around and look straight ahead at the blackboard. Walter had red hair and a small mouth. It seemed odd to have boys in my school.

We spent Christmas that year at Lake Tahoe, at a ski resort in the Sierra Mountains. To get there, we drove on snow-packed roads, with chains attached to the car tires, which made the ride go, thunk, thunk, thunk. The newly built Squaw Valley Lodge, a simple, rustic structure, had a big reception room with a high ceiling and exposed wooden beams. It had a large stone fireplace and always a cozy fire burning. Even with its warmth and decorations, I felt the emptiness of not being in New York with my father. I missed him.

The new ski resort had one chair lift and two rope tows. I wore rented skis and never managed to master the rope tow without falling down, but did enjoy the beginner ski class. I made a friend named Dickie LeMaire, whose father was a U.S. Olympic figure skater. We sledded and built snow forts together. (A decade later, many of the members of the U.S. Figure Skating Team would be killed in a plane crash flying across the Atlantic Ocean to Europe. Dickie and his father were on that plane.)

The next thing I knew, we were returning to New York. This time we flew on a noisy, comfortable plane with big propellers. I gave my turtle to Francie. We got to move back to our apartment on 72nd Street, which felt empty with just the three of us, but I got to see my father again, which made me happy. Mother enrolled in a six-week secretarial course.

I was back at Chapin in April, feeling settled in my familiar school. (My grandparents paid our tuition.) A project was underway, which happened for every third grade class – the creation of a mural depicting the sale of Manhattan Island to Peter Minuit from the Indians. Tina was my partner, and our job was to paint a picture of a Mayflower-type vessel sailing down the East River. Together we started with the hull, and life went on.

*The world, as I see it.*

# 2

## EARLY SUMMER

### 1955

HERE I AM ON the porch steps, tilting my face to the morning sun. I've taken off my navy blue Keds, white cotton socks, and cardigan sweater. Holley is upstairs with Helen, my cousin, in the bedroom they share. I hear their voices coming from an open window. All they do is talk. They whisper late at night, causing my mother or Aunt Ellie to keep going in to tell them to be quiet and go to sleep. How can there be so much to say?

Near me on the lawn, Helen's brother Dicky bounces a tennis ball up and down off his racket, working toward 100 bounces. Dicky is 12, and I'm about to be. My birthday is June 21st, which annoys me, because I never get to have a party with my school friends in New York. Here, on the rocky coast of Narragansett, Rhode Island, I don't have any friends, other than my cousins. Holley and Helen are 15.

Yesterday, my mother, Aunt Ellie, Dicky, and I, drove up from New York City to open the house for the summer. We arrived in a rented black Chevrolet. Both mothers have jobs as secretaries. Since we can't all fit in one car, Holley and Helen took the train from Grand Central Station to Kingston. My father was there to help them find seats. (Our fathers are not coming at all. They each have a new wife. Because Uncle Dick and Aunt Ellie got divorced a year before my parents, I thought this was a standard of marriage. You have a mother and a father, then the father leaves. My mother's friend called them 'scoundrels.')

In a week or so our trunks will arrive by Railway Express. The car trip, about 6 hours, went along Route 1 from New York to Connecticut and into Rhode Island, through towns, traffic lights, and past farms and cow pastures. We stopped at one Howard Johnson's for lunch, and another later on, for ice cream.

Known as "Flat Rock Cottage," the house was built in 1868 for my great-great grandfather, Francis Wharton, who came up summers from Washington, D.C. He was a lawyer, changed his mind, and went to divinity school in Cambridge, Massachusetts to become an Episcopal priest. Then he went back to being a lawyer. When he was living in Cambridge he became friends with Joseph Peace Hazard, who owned farmland in Narragansett and sold him this property. Dr. Wharton, as he was called, built this three-story, shingled "cottage," as well as a smaller house next door. The houses have remained in our family ever since.

Our grandparents own the two houses but they don't come much. Probably too hectic for them. When they do visit, they always take us to Aunt Carrie's, a local seafood restaurant, for dinner. They give this house to their two daughters and four grandchildren to use, and the one next door they rent to make money for upkeep. As soon as "Flat Rock" is set up for the season, one of our mothers will go back to the city and work, while the other stays with us. Then, in August, they'll switch places.

Every time I arrive at the house, my mind absorbs the scenery that I haven't seen for eight months. The lawn, the ocean, the hydrangea bushes. The tires crunch over the gravel driveway. Once the front door is unlocked I am instantly struck by the smell of damp musty air. This is one of my favorite summer memories.

When we've finished unloading the car, the next thing I do is tour the rooms, touching, remembering. I walk through, room by room: the parlor with an uncomfortable Victorian settee, that odd sofa in the hall with wooden pineapple posts. I check on the desktop with a cut-glass inkwell and the marble paperweight with a picture of the Roman Coliseum. Great-great grandfather's books are arranged as they've always been, probably unopened for sixty years. *Gibbon's History of the Roman Empire, Volumes I - VIII.* Trailing my hand along the banister, running upstairs, I check on the children's books, my mother's from childhood, and mine: *McDuffy's Eclectic Reader, Hans Brinker* or the *Silver Skates, The Lion the Witch and the Wardrobe.*

Now, in the kitchen, my mother and her sister unpack cartons of groceries left on the back porch from Ideal Market. They make lists. One of them will go to the phone company office to have the telephone turned on. The What Cheer laundry pick-up service needs to get started. Someone from Wakefield Branch Gas is scheduled to check the pilot light on the hot water heater, which won't stay lit. We still use the old-fashioned ice box on the back porch for extra space. A big block of ice will be delivered from the ice house in town, and we can put in lettuce and soft drinks. A plumber had come earlier in the week to turn on the water (rusty at first) and make sure everything worked.

On this brilliant June morning, the doors and windows are opened wide to let in the warm, dry air and release the trapped dampness that's been in the house since September. Buttercups dot the grass. The sun on my face feels delicious, especially after last night's torture of getting into a bed with freezing sheets. Like plunging into the cold ocean, you either go fast to get it over with, or go the cowardly way and do it slowly, which I did. Wearing socks helped a little. Before bed, we cousins played Parcheesi, then Sorry. It's a wonder how those tiny specks of insects survive in a cardboard box so many months, but there they are, scurrying, not happy with the bright light.

As soon as Dicky reaches 100 bounces with the tennis ball, we are going to take a rock walk to the "village," as we call the town of Narragansett. Our mothers no longer bother to warn us to, "Stay away from the slippery parts near the edge." By now we understand the dangers of the surf. The exhilaration instilled by this walk stuns me, not from exertion, but from the magnificence of the view. I recognize grandeur. From the end of the lawn, stone steps take me to the granite cliffs, then a left turn, and we'll walk a half mile along the coast to Monahan's Dock. Similar to rediscovering the interior of the house after the winter, I rediscover the rocks. There is the huge boulder plopped on top of all the pink granite. There's the one rock shaped like a piece of pie. Some parts of the surface have flat expanses that are easy to walk on, until a deep drop appears. Like mountain goats, Dicky and I, running, leap across the drops to the other side, where the rocks flatten again, then we run some more, jumping from level to level. Some places require a sharp descent and a rigorous climb to the next part.

Once we reach Monahan's Dock, we'll walk along the sea wall to the village and buy comics and candy at Weibel's news. *Little Lulu* for me, horror comics for Dicky. We walk back home on Ocean Road. Holley and Helen play Johnny Mathis records left from the summer before.

## 2018

No more mountain goat. I don't go to the rocks that much; descending the granite steps isn't easy. When I do get down there, I'll walk to the left for a bit, then there's the place that drops sharply to a lower level. I'll sit on my rear end, stretch out one leg then the other, and ease myself gently so I don't jolt my knees or twist an ankle. But the picture of the pink granite cliffs, with a bright morning sun reflecting off the ocean's ripples, and a clear blue sky, is a permanent postcard in my mind from childhood.

Now belonging to my sister, Flat Rock Cottage has heat, is used year-round, and in summers is filled with her children and grandchildren. The Victorian furniture survives, grouped around a flat screen TV. *Gibbon's History of the Roman Empire* hasn't moved from the shelf. On the children's shelves two more generations have been added alongside *McDuffy's Eclectic Reader*: *Charlie and the Chocolate Factory* and *Harry Potter*.

How the property was divvied up worked. After our mother remarried, she was able to afford the maintenance of the Narragansett houses. My grandparents gave her the property; Aunt Ellie got money, which she preferred. Then, as life went on with inheritance and such, Holley wanted the big house, and I liked the smaller one next door, so there it is. Our grandchildren are the 7th generation in the picture. Who knows what'll happen next. Will great-grandchildren run along the rocky shore to the sea wall? It is probable the two houses will be divided into two separate lots. There are real estate taxes and upkeep to consider. I understand this. Whatever changes, there will always be the magnet of the pink granite coast.

# It Was Just One of Those Things

*I learn to ballroom dance.*

# 3

## A Trip to the Moon on Gossamer Wings

"**B**ACK-SIDE-TOGETHER, FRONT-SIDE-TOGETHER, back-side-together, front-side-together. Don't look down, look straight ahead, over your partner's right shoulder. Girls, your left hand rests lightly on the boy's shoulder. Elbows are out, hold them straight. Boys, your right hand stays at the middle of the girl's back."

Mr. DeRham weaves his way through dancing couples – through the girls and boys struggling with the fundamentals of the box step. He straightens a girl's elbow here, a boy's posture there.

"Smile, Master Whitman, this isn't torture. Miss Wall, stop staring at your feet. You must follow the boy's lead."

Look at me: I am ten years old. I am wearing my new party dress from Best and Company. It is white organdy, with pink smocking, pink rosebuds at the collar, and a pink satin sash tied in a bow at the back of my waist. The sash has come untied. Robbie Whitman's sweaty palm has tugged the satin bow loose, leaving the ribbon dangling to the floor. The white cotton glove on my right hand has turned gray from Robbie's tight grip. He does look miserable; I feel sorry for him. I try to get him to talk. This is what I'm supposed to do. We are told by Mr. DeRham we should have conversations with our partners while we dance. I ask Robbie if he is a Yankees fan or a Dodgers fan. His face brightens, as he spews forth with much enthusiasm that he is a Yankees fan; he hates those Brooklyn bums. Just last week his grandfather took him and his brother to see the Yanks play the Boston Red Sox when it was raining, and he didn't care because they had really good box seats, and he ate two and a half hot dogs and Mickey Mantle hit a grand slam in the first inning. By now Robbie is jumping to the music, hopping up and down, stepping on my feet. That's all it takes. The Yankees.

When I ask what a grand slam is, he takes a deep breath, ready to explain in detail, only Mrs. DeRham has lifted the phonograph needle and stopped the music. Mr. DeRham calls out "double cut," meaning you change partners with the couple nearest you. There is always pushing and gentle shoving when this happens, as you try to end up next to someone you'd like to dance with. Sometimes the boys push and shove to dance with me, which is always exciting.

Dancing class feels good after worrying about my school work all day. I like dressing up. To get ready for class I dash from the Chapin bus to our apartment on 72$^{nd}$ Street, drop off my dreaded homework, have milk and cookies, brush my hair, and get into my party dress. Our part-time maid, Mary Greene, is there to help. She has my dress ironed, my black patent leather Mary Janes and fancy socks set out on a chair. She tries to untangle my hair without too much pulling. It is too curly and thick to wear hair ribbons or barrettes, but I always have hope. The barrettes spring off, and the ribbons don't hold. I want hair like Alice in Wonderland's, velvet headband and all. My hair doesn't grow long, only wide.

Mary Greene takes the bus down from Harlem in the afternoons to help with housekeeping and laundry and prepare supper while my mother is at the Moon Secretarial School. A comfortable and reassuring presence, Mary irons in the kitchen while she listens to soap operas on the radio. She loves Nat King Cole. As far as I know, I am the only fifth grader whose mother works. One friend also has divorced parents, but she has a stepfather. Another girl's mother died. I think she'd been sick, but that is something we never talk about. Then I have a friend whose father was killed in the war. She wears his "dog tags" on a chain around her neck, over her school uniform.

My mother needs to work. I know she doesn't get enough money from my father every month to support us. I learned about "alimony" when I heard her talking to my aunt on the phone. I don't want to hear these conversations, and if I do, I go to my room, shut the door, and have a stuffed animal tea party.

In order to get a job, Mother is taking a 6-week course run by the "wicked Miss Moon." She learns Gregg Shorthand – a form of mysterious loops and squiggles that make no sense. In the evenings she practices taking dictation on her steno pad while Holley or I read aloud from a workbook: "Dear Mr. Jones, In regards to your letter of January 17th..." After the course, she hopes to find a job in an interesting office.

To get to dancing school I take a private bus. At dusk I can see the street lamps along Park Avenue light up in succession: bing, bing, bing, bing, all the way down to where they end at Grand Central Station. The bus ride is hardly soothing, but it does have a certain sense of adventure. The fifth-grade boys in their blue suits, white shirts, and neckties, roughhouse and throw spitballs at each other. They climb over the backs of the seats and wrestle. Some have pea-shooters. The girls sit together, talking and talking the way girls do. Because most of us attend all-girls' or all-boys' schools around the city, being with girls causes the boys to act noisy and boisterous. Spit balls and peashooters perhaps are a ten-year-old's version of peacocks preening their feathers. Here I am. Here I am. On the other hand, we girls eye them with interest from our peripheral vision.

Class takes place in the ballroom of the Colony Club on Park Avenue and 62nd Street. The club, a four-story brick building, has white columns on the front. A doorman opens the heavy black doors and lets us in. Directly inside there is a great hall with marble floors, huge oriental rugs, and crystal chandeliers. Even the boys are hushed by the formality of the brilliant entryway after a ride in the dark interior of a spitball-zinging bus. After punch and cookies are served by volunteer mothers, each girl will be chosen by a boy to be his dance partner. The child-couples walk up, one by one, to where Mr. and Mrs. DeRham stand in the center of the ballroom. The boys bow, the girls curtsy. We then sit on gilt chairs that line the walls. I cross my ankles and keep my hands folded in my lap, as required. We are not allowed to rest our feet on the rungs of the chairs, which means your crossed ankles dangle into space. This is not comfortable. The final couples to enter are usually girls with girls – since they always outnumber the boys. In fact, there is a waiting list of girls to join the class, while the boys are offered a reduced fee.

A portable record player resembling a suitcase sits on top of the piano. Mrs. DeRham lowers the phonograph needle into a groove of a record and wafts over to her husband. Standing before him, they fall into position and glide across the floor in a smooth foxtrot. "It was just one of those things, just one of those wonderful things…"

She wears taffeta dresses with full skirts that swish back and forth as she sways to the music. Her shriveled cleavage, just about eye-level to a fifth grade boy, is revealed by low-cut necklines. Mr. DeRham is impeccable in his dark suit, except for the dandruff on his shoulders. Strands of oily Vitalised hair are carefully combed over his balding head. He smells like cigarettes. They dance gracefully, even when demonstrating the basic box-step. We stand up and face our partner and mimic the instructors. Back-side-together. Front-side-together. At arm's length, we stiffly perform the box step. I find the whole thing rather thrilling.

Some kids hate dancing school. My chubby friend gets stomach aches and often hides in the ladies room the entire session. Not me. I am out there eying those cute boys.

Philip, in particular. He is tall and has blue eyes and good posture. Except for a cowlick, his light brown hair has a part that looks like it was made with a ruler. Philip knows how to hold a girl firmly at her back. He is one of Mrs. DeRham's favorites, and she picks him to be her partner a lot. (He never looks happy about it.) Sometimes he dances with me. "A trip to the moon, on gossamer wings…" Even at age ten I recognize how satisfying it is to dance with a boy who knows how to lead.

At the end of class we get to do "The Mexican Hat Dance," an athletic sort of dance where everyone can release their stifled energy and act goofy. Like a square dance, we line up on two sides and don't have to be with a particular partner. Hooking arms, we spin faster and faster, then switch directions, until my head throbs from dizziness and I have to sit down. This is a relief after an evening of good manners.

The mothers and fathers pick us up at 6:00. I can see my mother in the viewing gallery, talking with other parents. To me she always seems distracted, probably tired and worried. But she smiles and asks if I had a good time. We take a taxi to the apartment, where we have chicken and peas left warming for us by Mary Greene. My mother will hang up my wrinkled organdy dress while I take a bath and get into my pajamas. There is still homework – spelling and arithmetic. They have to wait for the ride on the school bus in the morning. "…Just one of those things…"

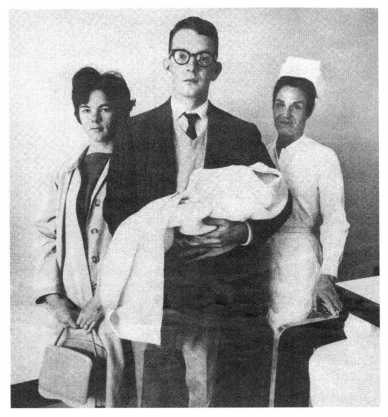

*Advertisement for Metropolitan Life Insurance
published in Life Magazine, 1967.*

# 4

## METROPOLITAN LIFE

YES, THAT'S ME ON the left, 23 and posing as a new mother. Pretending to be the father was a man hired from a "real people" model agency in Manhattan. They supplied the nurse as well. The photographer was Diane Arbus, a name that meant nothing to me in 1967. So how did I wind up on the last page of *Life Magazine*?

At the time this advertisement for Metropolitan Life Insurance was produced, I worked for Young and Rubicam Advertising. "Y&R" took up 16 floors of an art-deco office building at 285 Madison Avenue, between 40th and 41st Streets in New York City. I was in "styling," a part of the art department. The five stylists (I being the youngest and lowliest), were responsible for selecting outfits that models and actresses wore in print advertisements and TV commercials. It was a glamorous and exciting job.

We'd hail taxis to 7th Avenue (on expense accounts) to visit designer showrooms. The publicity worked well for them; they were eager to loan their creations. Seagram's Whiskey or Chrysler advertisements required the most elegant outfits: long evening gowns worn by bejeweled models. I mostly searched Gimbels and Macy's for dresses to be worn by housewives while they cheerfully mopped kitchen floors with Spic and Span. Always dresses.

We, as stylists, selected our own outfits to coincide with current trends. The fashion image was good for the agency. I wore mini skirts and white vinyl boots up to my knees. Our department head wore designer suits, two inches above the knee. That was the style, everything short. The hairdos were a motionless bouffant. My stubborn curls overruled the sprayed and teased "do" which never stayed smooth for me.

One piece of apparel not yet seen in print was the "pantsuit." It was creeping into the fashion scene, an avant-garde concept of a tailored woman's suit but with pants instead of a skirt. *Women's Wear Daily* wrote about them, though they were far from mainstream. On a dare from us, a colleague showed up one day in a navy twill Oleg Cassini design: a double-breasted jacket and pants. Walking down the corridor, almost like a runway, past the rows of desks and secretaries, she received cheers and applause. "Hooray! You did it!" we all exclaimed.

The day of the Met Life photo-shoot started out like any other: I was typing expense reports. Meanwhile, on the executive floor, a discussion was in progress with the photographer, the art director, and the client. Diane Arbus was not satisfied with the "young mother" provided by the "real people" modeling agency and sent her home. A replacement had to be found quickly, as everything else was set to go. Ms. (a newly-invented word) Arbus and the Y&R creative team walked the corridors in search of possibilities.

Working at my desk, I was distracted by murmuring nearby. When I looked up, I realized the group was talking about me. One woman gave a subtle nod in my direction and said, "She'd be good."

I wondered what I'd be good for. With approval by the team, approval by my boss, and consent from me, I was plucked from behind my IBM typewriter, and the next thing I knew I was heading to the location of the shoot – New York Presbyterian Hospital. I did not know I was riding in a taxi with a foremost internationally-acclaimed photographer with works exhibited in major museums all over the world. But I was pretty happy with how my day was going.

I recall that I was wearing a short, A-line, brown linen dress, a favorite. Because Ms. Arbus liked authenticity and needed an apprehensive new mom and not a hip New York stylist, she had me wear a dowdy raincoat, borrowed from a hospital employee, over my fashionable dress. That was disappointing. She staged me this way and that with the "nurse" and my husband-of-the-hour. He was told to look anxious about forthcoming responsibilities and held a doll wrapped in a baby blanket.

While I was concentrating on fashion trends in 1966, the Vietnam War was raging at full momentum. My real husband and I had friends in places like Danang and Saigon. Some we kept in touch with by mail. When the Met Life ad ran, I received two letters from overseas, asking: "Is that you, Camilla, in *Life Magazine*? Who's that man? Where's Charlie?"

An understandable question since we'd been married in 1966. In my mind I can see our first apartment at 306 East 96th Street, between 1st and 2nd Avenues, a new high-rise building in a land of 4-story walk-ups and electrical supply stores. The 11th floor apartment faced south, with a vista all the way to the Chrysler building on 33rd Street. At night the New York skyline looked like a picture postcard. Northward, the neighborhoods turned into housing projects and scrap metal yards.

After four years, my enthusiasm for my artsy and sophisticated career flagged. The work was more often about searching for cabs in the rain and schlepping bags loaded with cast iron casseroles and other table props for food commercials...or returning house dresses to Macy's that weren't used. Walking home from the subway tired me. The next chapter beckoned.

As if following a script, I became pregnant; Charlie and I left Manhattan for a rented house in Westchester County. Of the Met Life advertisement I only have this one page, torn from the magazine, which I recently came across while going through file boxes. An event completely forgotten, the memory has come back as a ripply scene in an old movie flashback.

*View from 'Victoria Peak' of Hong Kong, showing our May Tower apartment building, 1977.*

*Same view, 2018.*

# 5

## WE MOVE TO HONG KONG, 1977

WHEN WE WERE IN our thirties, my husband Charlie and I moved to the Royal Crown Colony of Hong Kong with our sons, Chris and John. The boys, six and eight, were fine with the move. After all, it had only been a year since we moved from Providence to Boston. They were familiar with packers, cardboard boxes, and the enormous moving van. As long as their toys re-appeared at the other end. We carefully studied pictures of the city, the harbor, and the catalogue for the Hong Kong International School. The move would be hard work, but exciting. I looked forward to world travel.

As a boy, Charlie grew up overseas. Employed by Alcan, a Canadian aluminum company, his father was transferred from country to country. The family lived in London; Montreal; Sao Paolo, Brazil; and Cali, Colombia. Years later, the stories – legends – were told and retold at Thanksgiving and Christmas dinner tables. Charlie's mother, Granny Lee, related the time Charlie and his brother Phip threw a lamp at the burglar climbing through a window in Brazil. Or how in 1953 they watched the coronation of Queen Elizabeth II from a London sidewalk. As I grew up only in New York City, the stories intrigued me. Now our family would continue the expatriate tradition.

My husband was in the investment business. The reason we moved our family from Boston to Hong Kong was that his employer at the time, PaineWebber, asked if he'd be interested in opening an Asian branch office. Because of his overseas background, he was a natural choice, a person with a sense of adventure. The idea was enticing. And Hong Kong especially, famous for mystique and glitter, added to our curiosity.

We did not anticipate the added component of living through a significant time in history. Across the border, the People's Republic of China (the PRC), was permitting foreigners into their country for the first time since 1912. During our stay, the Romanization of the Chinese language, a system founded by the British in 1867, became obsolete. The city that was named "Canton" by foreigners lost its English name and became, rightfully, Guangzhou. "Peking" became Beijing.

Our adventure began on the fastest route Pan American Airlines could offer, from Boston to San Francisco to Honolulu to Tokyo and finally landing at Hong Kong's Kai Tak airport. Kai Tak, with an inadequate runway for the new jumbo jets, abutted residential neighborhoods in Kowloon, making for a dramatic approach. From the airplane window you could see laundry hanging on apartment house balconies.

Arriving in August, we spent our first week at the Hong Kong Hilton, where we waited for our furniture and tried not to be homesick. There were other expatriates staying at the hotel, also waiting for their shipments from overseas or looking for apartments. We met families working for Caterpillar Tractor, The National Bank of Dallas, and 3-M. Chris and John made friends with other American children in the coffee shop and by the pool. The Hilton doorman - a grandfatherly Indian in a turban – didn't mind having the kids linger around the entrance of the hotel, telling him about their homes in the States. They would ask him strings of questions: How many taxi doors did he open in one day? Did he ever go fishing? Had he been to America? (No, but he had a son at UCLA). When school opened in September, the bus for HKIS would drive under the portico and suck in eight to ten children. The numbers decreased as the families were settled.

We did not have to apartment hunt, as we were fortunate to have one waiting, one of the perks of my husband's employer. May Tower, a new building, solidly constructed to withstand mudslides and typhoons, was positioned half-way up Victoria Peak, the dramatic mountain rising from the center of Hong Kong Island. A duplex, our new home had large windows overlooking the Governor's Mansion, the Botanical Gardens, and in the distance, Hong Kong Harbor. The view of cruise ships and freighters, junks and sampans, was spectacular; but to see it from our balcony made you dizzy. Standing on the tenth floor of a building situated on a steep hill plays tricks with your equilibrium.

Our shipment of household goods arrived neatly and on schedule. The graceful Chinese movers padded around the apartment in white socks, placing furniture and cartons in appropriate spaces. A few days later, while unpacking linens, the back doorbell rang. At the doorway stood two visitors, an old man and a young woman. The man was Ah Ping, a houseboy, who was not a boy, but a wizened man who might have been in his sixties. I recognized him because I had met his employers – a British couple who lived high up on Victoria Peak - where the view was even more spectacular and the houses, not apartments, impressive. That's how the prestige ladder was structured – it worked its way up the mountain. (Except the top of the peak was often shrouded in clouds and mist.) I did not know the woman.

My husband and I had been to that couple's house for a party, where Ah Ping took our coats, our drink orders, and served dinner at a formally set table. Known in the expatriate community, he was senior man in procuring work for Chinese servants from whom he'd collect an employment fee. It was rumored that when Ah Ping was a young man living in Shanghai, he had sold one of his daughters. Selling girls into slavery was not uncommon at that time, in order to survive the famine of 1943. Now, here in my kitchen doorway, Ah Ping introduced me to the silent woman standing at his side, our potential servant.

"Very good, *amah*, Missee," he said, pointing to her, as though she were a new appliance. "Work very hard."

I liked Ah Fung's face with its hint of humor immediately. While she stood quietly to the side, Ah Ping and I discussed salary and Chinese holidays (of which there were many) in fractured English and hand-gestures. It was not until the end of negotiations that it was revealed Ah Fung had a son, Ah-Ming, who was in the picture as well. It was surprising news that an 11-year-old boy would be coming to live with us, but by that time it was too late for me to re-consider. You might say I was duped. It would not be the first time. In my mind, there was no room for another person. Although our flat was modern and gracious, the kitchen and amah's quarters were not. Ah Fung's room was the size of today's "walk-in closet."

The idea was, in 1977, that a servant who cooked, cleaned, washed and ironed, should be grateful to have a roof over her head. They would both sleep on a metal bunk bed in the tiny room.

The way I lived felt something like role-playing; I suddenly became the "mistress of the house." This is how mornings began: the dining room table, laid out for breakfast, had boxes of cereal, a pitcher of milk, and a copy of the *South China Morning Post* at Charlie's place. Slices of papaya and mango were arranged on a platter. Ah Fung, appearing from the kitchen, poured us coffee. "Master, Missee, wanchee loll toastee?" she might loudly ask. Translation: "Mr. and Mrs. Lee, would you like toast or a croissant?" The question was asked with the inflection of the Cantonese dialect that, to me, was unpleasantly grating.

After breakfast the morning rush ensued: searching for homework and jackets, signing a permission slip for a class trip to the sewage treatment plant or the new aquarium. Ah Fung had lunch bags ready as the boys ran to catch their HKIS school bus at a stop convenient to several apartment buildings. Then Master, I mean my husband, either took the Peak Tram – a funicular trolley built in the late 1800's – or I drove him down the hill to his office in "Central," the business district. Being an English colony, the Hong Kong traffic direction was backwards to me. We had a white Honda Civic, with the steering wheel on the right, a standard shift at my left, and blue leather upholstery. The round trip could take twenty minutes. After dropping Charlie off, I'd drive back up the steep incline to our apartment (a challenge with a standard-shift vehicle), and stay in the living room while Ah Fung made the beds and cleaned the rooms. I'd sit on the sofa and wonder what to do next.

Those first months were difficult. Although we'd moved several times – it felt different in Hong Kong. I anchored myself with an established routine, which was to create a sense of nesting as quickly as possible. This meant getting the furniture, pictures, and rugs, arranged in a familiar layout. The box of toys would be located and unpacked. In time, I'd attend to the rest of the cartons. But the strangeness – the language, the unreadable signs, the foreignness, made me long for home.

Arranging our lamps was a challenge as the apartment had few electrical outlets. I needed to purchase extension cords. Because Hong Kong was a British Colony, the wall sockets were British, although some were Chinese. The sockets came two-pronged, three pronged, large and small. Our lamps were American. I made a detailed list of what I needed, which lamp went with which outlet. On a mission, I took the Peak Tram downtown, in ninety-degree heat and oppressive humidity, and walked through the hazy, exhaust-filled streets of the city. The pollution made my eyes sting.

Central had narrow sidewalks and such a volume of pedestrian traffic, it was hard to maintain any sort of clear space around your body. I saw no recognizable hardware stores. Stopping to ask the doorman of the Mandarin Hotel, he directed me to a special alley of electrical supplies, about five blocks away. There I found a row of outdoor stalls dealing mainly with the assembly of custom-made extension cords. I chose the establishment of a man with a wide and toothless smile. Together we sketched a few diagrams: length of cord, prong size, etc. Cheerful and helpful, he made what I needed, but the effort of this one household errand depleted my energy. On that steamy, September day in 1977, I did not find the steep, cobble-stoned alley of electrical supply booths charming in its Chinese tradition, as I would later in my stay. It was frustrating and infuriating. The other task that day was to shop for a shower curtain, but instead I went to the Hilton coffee shop, had a grilled cheese sandwich, and took a taxi home.

I wanted to teach Ah Fung a correct, dignified English. I tried to have her call us "Mr. and Mrs. Lee," but she was not at all interested. The way she spoke was like a cliché from Charlie Chan movies – the ones now condemned for stereotyping. I did not like being called "Master and Missee." On the other hand, in her mind, "Master and Missee" might have been a translation for "Tweedle Dee and Tweedle Dum," or some Chinese derogatory term for goofy characters. The titles of respect were ambiguous.

Slender and friendly, Ah Fung wore cotton pants and tops that never matched – busy prints with other busy prints, or sometimes plaids. She slapped around the apartment in plastic flip-flops with pandas on them, dusting and humming. The classic older amahs were known as "black and whites," referring to the black pants and white tops they always wore. I did not care about uniforms, and Ah Fung, it seemed, had no intention of wearing one. Most domestic servants were older, but Ah Fung had other motives. Having her son live with a Western family for example. "You Americans are so lenient with your help," a British woman once told me at a charity luncheon, when I described my domestic situation.

I was grateful to have a Chinese amah. It was especially useful to have her communicate with the service people – repairmen and such. She loudly scolded them for tracking in dirt or making a mess with their tools (which they never did). But Ah Fung did it for show on my behalf, demonstrating she was in charge. Part of the Cantonese culture, I learned, involved yelling insults at each other, although it never amounted to anything. When she introduced me to her husband who came over one Saturday, she said: "This is my husband Missee, he is short and fat." He was short, but not fat. The family had an apartment in a resettlement block across the harbor in Kowloon, where her husband was a factory worker. The reason I emphasize *Chinese* amah, is because more and more families were employing young women from the Philippines to work in their households. These educated women, sometimes nurses or accountants, left a country where living conditions were deplorable and income meager. Their seemingly substantial Hong Kong salaries would be sent back to parents, husbands, and children.

The Chinese eyed the Filipinas with distrust. Ah Fung told me one day with certainty: "Filipina amah in 6-A no good. When missee go away, Filipina amah sleep with master." This was a fact she learned from the doorman.

Domestic service was losing momentum with the Chinese, as the next generation chose to work in factories and gain independence. There was a shift in culture. During our stay, the influx of Filipinas continued to grow. On Sundays, the domestics (not *amahs*) gathered downtown in "Statue Square," a municipal park that had once been an English cricket field. They'd fill the entire plaza, go to the Catholic Church, and socialize on their one day off. By our third year in Hong Kong, the Sunday gatherings of women were so dense, they flowed beyond the plaza, pressing against the historic British Hong Kong Club and the Mandarin Hotel. The Chinese were not happy with the increasing population.

Soon after the start of school, the rhythm of our week grew more comfortable, much like a school year back in the States. Halloween came, and the boys (Frankenstein and the Incredible Hulk), went trick-or-treating with friends. Ah Ming went along, dressed as Dracula with a cape and plastic fangs. Unfamiliar with the American custom of trick-or-treating, he seemed wary and uncomfortable as they traveled in a group from door-to-door in our building and others nearby. What Ah Ming thought of us I can hardly imagine. The boys and he played with GI Joes. They taught him to swim in the May Tower pool to the strong disapproval of other building residents. He would have been about 12, a year older than Chris, and was quick to learn.

Thanksgiving came and Butterball turkeys filled the freezers of the Western supermarkets. Cans of Ocean Spray cranberry sauce went on display. At Christmas, live balsam trees came from Canada in a special shipment offered by Pan Am. But the needles fell off as soon as they were removed from the air tight cargo hold. Some families had grandparents visit, a source of comfort and nostalgia, as there was a strange absence of anyone over fifty in the expatriate community.

With soccer and Cub Scouts, it could be home but with some significant changes. Unlike home with car-pooling, Chris and John could get around the city by themselves. There was a toy store across the harbor in Kowloon they might go to with friends on Saturdays. To get there they'd take the Peak Tram to Central, then walk a few blocks to the Star Ferry for the ride across the harbor. The ferries ran constantly, a twenty minute journey – the only way for pedestrians to cross the water. The main appeal of the toy store was the British-made metal tanks and other artillery it carried.

Also different was the lack of a play yard. Instead of a grassy area "out back," we had a vertical cliff with a waterfall cascading from the top of the peak. The scene was as dramatic as that in front of our apartment, downhill facing the harbor. On the cliff was a botanical nursery, where colorful pots of flowers were set along narrow steppes cut into the rock. Nursery men dipped and filled their watering cans in a concrete cistern filled by the falls. As in a 19th-century hand-tinted print, the workers balanced long bamboo poles across their shoulders – a vessel hanging from each end. In wide-brimmed hats, they climbed up and down from one level to the next, deftly watering the potted flowers. Yet the cliff was an exciting playground for the boys and their friends. Once Chris, playing Tarzan, broke his arm swinging to the ground from a scrawny tree. A thick, solid cast was applied by Dr. Wong, the orthopedic surgeon at Hong Kong Adventist Hospital. Years later I learned of other terrifying stunts the boys performed. Climbing around the outside of balconies was one.

I volunteered in the school library and joined The American Women's Association, the A.W.A., an organization that hosted fundraisers to support scholarships for Chinese students or to purchase equipment for the hospital. It offered classes, where I took needlepoint lessons and partially learned to play bridge.

My Hong Kong evenings were often not as relaxing as the days. At least two or three nights a week we went to dinner parties at expatriate homes to honor their bosses from the main office. The men came from New York and London to review the company's foreign branches. Their wives were invited too. Cocktails would be served by a houseboy – gin and tonics or scotch-on-the-rocks – ice clinking in crystal, subdued conversation. (Wine had not yet emerged as a cocktail beverage.) The atmosphere was strained.

Sometimes it was our turn to host, which for me, caused panic. I'd never been comfortable with entertaining, and this type of dinner, seated with place cards, raised my level of anxiety. Charlie, usually relaxed, was anxious as well as he fussed over the table seating or straightened furniture. A recipe from the "Joy of Cooking" for chicken Kiev became a standard that Ah Fung and I learned to master. Unlike me, she was interested in cooking and did it well. She'd sauté Bok choy in oil and lots of garlic, always popular and something foreign to our guests.

As for the presentation, I never knew what to expect from Ah Fung. Even though I pulled out my Wedgwood china and silver platter, the entree might appear in a disposable aluminum roasting pan. It was all the same to her. To help serve and wash up, an amah-friend came. From behind the kitchen door, sounds of clattering pots and pans, animated chatter and laughter would drown out the quiet and stilted conversation at my formal table. I was envious. Afterward, my jaw muscles hurt from the concentrated effort of smiling and being witty. Dinner parties were a requisite part of the job.

We lived in Hong Kong for three and a half years. Did I love it? I did not love the crowds, the humidity, the feeling of confinement. It was hard to be that far away from home and family. Yet the exotic climate of the Royal Crown Colony was intoxicating – the junks and sampans, the amahs, the British governor. It was the beginning of "Made in China," first silk and cloisonné, then knitwear. Some of the boys' toy tanks have survived, played with by grandchildren. Of course things have changed. Junks are no longer a system of transport. A new international airport was built on an outlying island with a bridge to the mainland. We used to go to that island, once a fishing village, by ferry and eat fresh seafood at ramshackle restaurants. Another development: a subway system has been installed. The Star Ferry is no longer *the* system of transport to cross the harbor, but more of a tourist ride. I do know I love looking back on those days. I have an etched memory of a fleet of junks under full batwing sail, ghosting into Hong Kong Harbour bearing cargo from the People's Republic of China.

The good friends I made in Hong Kong remain my good friends today. Grandmothers now, we keep in touch by email and laugh over anecdotes of our expatriate lives. It was two lifetimes ago. I have photographs, small and faded, reminding me of a time long past. The memories float up easily and make my eyes go damp.

*Ah Fung's journey from Hong Kong to Lo Wu and the Chinese Border.*

# 6

## AH FUNG GOES TO LO WU

I KNOW IT WAS WEDNESDAY, 9:00 AM; I see myself getting ready to leave the apartment and drive to the Hong Kong International-al School - HKIS, where I volunteered in the middle school library. Chris and John were in the sixth and fourth grades. I remember searching for my car keys in the dragon bowl on the hall table. The Chinese bowl held a tangle of keys, rubber bands, plastic army men, and other flotsam. Ah Fung had already made the beds, dusted the furniture, and cleaned the bathrooms. Her pace did seem accelerated that day, although I didn't think much of it at the time. Only later in retrospect. Retrieving the car keys, I started to open the front door, when she came out to stop me.

"Missee, ok I go Lo Wu see sister. She coming China. Be back six o'clockee."

She was asking if she could take the day off to go meet her sister, who was coming over from China. She would take the train from Kowloon, north to the farthermost end of The New Territories, right before the checkpoint to the People's Republic of China.

"Of course you can go," I replied. It seemed a sudden impulse, to see her sister. But that was ok. It wasn't as though I couldn't manage without an amah for a day.

Lo Wu was an active market town, with a large and busy railroad station. It was part of the Royal Crown Colony of Hong Kong. The geography went like this, going from south to north: Hong Kong Island (where we lived), Victoria Harbour, and across the harbor, the Kowloon Peninsula. Then came a 400-square mile expanse of land known simply as the New Territories, a tract that was part of a 99-year lease Great Britain had signed with China in1898. Eighty years later (when we were there), the territory was hardly new, but the name hadn't changed. The Lo Wu border separated communism from democracy. Ah Fung's sister lived across the border.

Recently the visitation rules had relaxed, and with proper documents, families from China could take the train into Lo Wu and spend the day with their Hong Kong relatives. They would bring gifts of herbal medicines, moon cakes, and ground rhinoceros horn (a Chinese version of Viagra). In turn, the Hong Kong residents sent them home with Sony televisions, Swiss chocolates, and American laundry soap. Although I'd never been there, I imagined an open market filled with vegetables and fish, woks and baskets, red plastic buckets, live snakes for special dinners, finches in bamboo cages, toilet paper, and squawking chickens. But other than a few towns, most of the New Territories was primitive and agricultural, as it must have been for a century. It is likely that some inhabitants were unaware of the bustling city of Hong Kong, just an hour away, bursting with high rise buildings and bright neon signs advertising wristwatches and cigarettes. They couldn't have dreamed of the fancy apartments with exotic kitchen appliances, outlandish bathrooms, and so many white foreigners.

For us, the New Territories served as a peaceful weekend outing where we could hike on the trails of the recently established conservation land. From Hong Kong we'd drive through the newly-built Cross Harbour Tunnel, then through the congested streets of Kowloon, past Kai Tak Airport. Even after three years of residency, my heart stopped whenever a jumbo jet flew low across the road, coming in from the mountains for a landing. It seemed as though the wings would catch the drying laundry skewered on poles from shabby apartment houses. Like banners at a festival, the bamboo poles stuck straight out from balconies: underwear, towels, pajamas, fully on display. (Fifteen years later, in 1998, the airport was relocated to an outlying island, replacing a fishing village, while a 1-mile bridge connected it to Hong Kong. Of course the new airport was large and efficient, but many residents missed the inadequate Kai Tak, an icon of the former British Colony.)

Beyond Kowloon, the traffic decreased and the scenery turned pastoral, as though changing from black and white to Technicolor. We would drive past rice paddies, duck farms, and vegetable crops plowed by water buffalo. Hunched over in the fields, native *Hakka* women harvested the crops. They wore the traditional, wide-brimmed straw hats edged with a four-inch drop of black fabric, to block the sun. The hat was a cultural style, 200 years old. Driving perhaps an hour on the only road, we'd reach a small, sandy parking lot at the trailhead to Mirs Bay. There we would disembark with our picnic lunch (prepared by Ah Fung), and walk two miles to a beach accessible only on foot or by boat. Along the trail we'd come to an isolated village tucked into a hill. The dwellings, made of stucco and mud, were attached side-to-side as in a strip mall. Ceramic tiles on the roofs provided color. There were dirt floors, old people with few teeth, and no plumbing or electricity. We'd walk by, cheerily calling *"jo san"* (good morning). Smiling broadly, the villagers would *"jo san"* back, as they went about their business of pumping well-water into buckets for the daily washing. The trail ended farther along, at a precipice, where the view stretched beyond the blue-green water of Mirs Bay to a series of islands belonging to Mainland China. A perfect spot for our picnic. Sometimes we'd see a fleet of Chinese junks, rigged with faded red sails, making their way to Hong Kong.

*Junk sailing into Mirs Bay - photo by Charles Lee.*

I was glad that Ah Fung had the opportunity to see her sister. She was her only sibling; there had been a brother who died. He had drowned in

Mirs Bay, while swimming from China to Hong Kong, trying to escape the dictatorship of Mao Tse-tung. The beliefs of the glorified Chairman Mao had become murky. During the mid-sixties, thousands of people were escaping from China, piling into The New Territories every day. Getting past the border patrol was frightening and perilous. They hid in rural villages and gradually moved to the city, sleeping in alleys and doorways. Compact little domiciles appeared on rooftops. There were lean-tos made from tarps, with camping stoves and clotheslines. By the time we moved to Hong Kong, ten years later, most of the refugees had been settled into massive and industrial-looking apartment developments. Some found jobs in factories or restaurant kitchens. Others, like Ah Fung, went into domestic service. (Today, most of the farmland of the New Territories has become fancy housing developments with names like Beverly Hills and Grand View Gardens.)

Driving to my library duty at the school, I pondered Ah Fung's request. It was more of an announcement: "Missee I go Lo Wu see sister." I thought about it as I navigated around the bends of the hills of Magazine Gap Road. At morning rush hour the narrow winding road was congested, but I was heading out of the city with plenty of space on my side. I drove the Honda Civic, down-shifting, up-shifting, confident about the British driving arrangements which now felt natural. Apartment buildings, many under construction, had replaced private houses. One particular residence however, Grecian in character, still stood on a knoll facing the bay, abandoned, except for squatters' laundry hanging out to dry. I am a sucker for nostalgia and could conjure rich British merchants taking tea on the veranda, served by houseboys with long queues (pigtails).

The Hong Kong International School, 10 miles outside of the city, was situated on the side of a hill overlooking the bright water of Repulse Bay (an area once used as a summer retreat for expatriates). Administered by the Lutheran Church of America, most students were from the United States, but many were from elsewhere; Chris and John had friends from the Netherlands to Sri Lanka to Scotland. My duties in the library involved working on circulation and shelving. Mostly, I liked getting to know the students and the teachers.

When school was over that day, I drove the boys home, stopping for ice cream along the way. I had forgotten about Ah Fung's trip to Lo Wu. When we got back to the apartment, it seemed empty, until I saw the kitchen light go on through a small window in the swinging door.

Ah Fung came through and said, "I very sorry Missee; my sister give me her girl."

Standing next to her, holding her hand, was a very small child with short cropped hair and black eyes, looking at me, scared. I might have been the first foreign person she had ever seen, other than on her short journey to Hong Kong. She was five years old.

Stunned, my mind raced, wondering if this was just a visit or a more permanent stay. Of course it was permanent; why else would Ah Fung be slipping off to Lo Wu? The event had surely been in the planning stages for weeks. The promising city of Hong Kong offered vast opportunities.

"What do you mean?" I asked. "What do you mean, 'she gave you her girl'? We don't have space for another child. There's hardly space in the bunk beds for you and Ah Ming." (Her son had turned twelve.)

"Ah Ming sleep top, girl and me sleep down," she said, matter-of-factly.

Feeling totally taken advantage of, I was angry and flustered. I didn't want another child in the apartment. Ah Fung, an opportunist, had tricked me again. After all, she duped me at the start of her employ by bringing a son with her. "I don't know what Master is going to say," I added, trying to act threatening with the mention of my husband. Then I asked, looking down at this small, quiet person, "What's her name?" I was trying to contain my fury.

"Ah Gnoh," she replied. Translation: Little Goose. The Chinese could choose the most demeaning nicknames.

I was speechless; my thoughts cleared. Here was this tiny human being who had been handed over by her mother to her auntie, as though she was a new quilt. And she hardly knew her auntie, Ah Fung. They would only meet once a year at Chinese New Year. This child came from a place where girls did not go to school. They were meant to cook and clean, bear sons, and take care of their elders. Newborn girls often ended up in orphanages, or worse. Kneeling down, I lowered myself to Little Goose's height.

"Hello," I said gently. "Welcome to Hong Kong." She was motionless.

Later, when Charlie came home from work, all business-like, with his briefcase, I sat on the bed and told him of the day's event with Ah Fung and the trip to Lo Wu. His response was indignant.

"There's no way we can have another child in the apartment. This is ridiculous! She has to go. She could go to a cousin in Kowloon. Aren't there cousins there? I'll go have a word with Ah Fung."

Hanging up his suit, he got into his evening costume of soft cotton khakis and a sweater, and stalked to the kitchen.

Little Goose was sitting at the table with a bowl of rice in front of her, saying nothing, not eating. So far, she had not said a word. Ah Ming had come back from school and was sitting next to her, doing his homework. He chatted with his mother while she busied about, washing dishes. When my husband went in, I could hear his voice, brusque, official. The conversation evened out, and I could hear him talking to Ah Ming about school. His voice grew quieter, and the conversation fell into murmurings.

After about twenty minutes, Charlie came back to the living room. "We need to get the girl some proper shoes," he said. "She can't go around in those slipper-things."

After a few days, Ah Fung asked me if I had any ideas on what to name Little Goose. It was the custom of the educated Chinese, the new generation, to have a Christian name, in addition to their native one. Like naming a puppy from the animal shelter, we discussed it as a family and chose the name Mary. I wanted to keep it simple and classic, avoiding names like Kimberly or Ashley.

Mary remained mostly on a small stool at the kitchen table for three weeks, without speaking.

"She no talkee," Ah Fung said, concerned.

She followed Ah Fung around the apartment, studying the furniture with curiosity, cautiously observing Chris and John play noisily with their GI Joes and Matchbox cars. The boys gave her candy and coloring books.

Then one day I heard a soft voice out in the kitchen. Mary had said something! Over the next few days she said more things. In a few weeks she was talking non-stop. We cheered as she chatted on and on. Ah Fung got her a Barbie doll with long, gold hair and a bright pink dress. Mary dressed and undressed her. Ah Fung's friends brought more Barbie outfits.

She earnestly worked on the sticker books and puzzles we gave her. I worried about her education. About the fact that there wasn't any plan.

Chinese children begin school at three years old, when they start learning their characters. There are hundreds of characters in Chinese writing. Mary was already five and had never been to school. It seemed an impossibility to enroll her anywhere. Nor had anyone mentioned education. So I hired a tutor – a friend of a teacher at school, to come twice a week in our apartment. The young woman was humorless and Mary squirmed through the lessons, wanting to get back to her fresh pile of toys. But her education was off to a start.

Two months later we would relocate back to the United States, to a suburb of Boston. Ah Fung got another job, a day job. She and Ah Ming and Mary moved to an apartment in Kowloon where Ah Fung could be with her husband, a man she rarely saw.

Now in 2018, Mary would be 44, Ah Ming 52? After we left Hong Kong, I sent Ah Fung a letter, telling her about our trip home. Ah Ming could have translated it for her. Only the letter came back, no such address. Ah Fung had my address, but she never wrote. Rather, she never got Ah Ming to write for her. I would give anything to know where they are now.

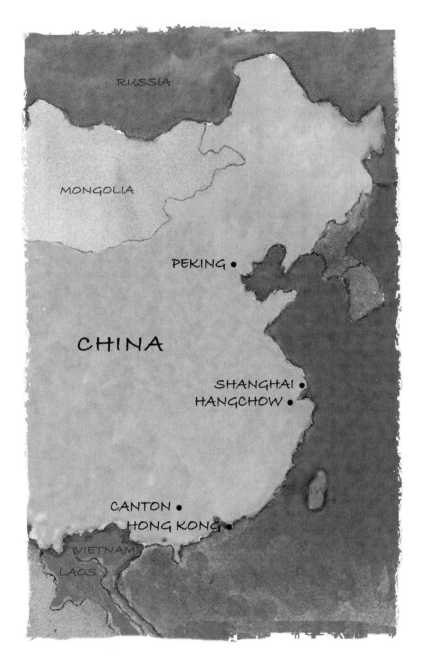

*The China Travel Service itinerary from Canton to Peking.*

# 7

## TRIP TO CHINA, 1979

IN 1979, OUR SECOND year in Hong Kong, Charlie and I took a 10-day trip to the People's Republic of China, the PRC. I'd kept a journal of our trip, which got lost during the packing and unpacking of our moves over the next 30 years. Now I found it. It was stored in a box of Charlie's report cards his mother had saved, not in the box marked "travel journals." Also stored with my journal was the only available guidebook at the time, *The Guide to China, 1979,* published by the China Travel Service. This is the preface:

> ### THE CHINA GUIDEBOOK
>
> DEDICATED
> to the promise of enhanced
> understanding among nations
> on the occasion of the establishment
> of full diplomatic relations
> between the People's Republic of China
> and the United States of America.

I didn't know I was a writer, so much of the China journal entries are sadly lacking in detail. "We had a wonderful meal." "The hotel was wonderful." There are a lot of "wonderfuls." But the story is there, the story of China's start as a tourist destination and world power. The revered communist leader, Mao-Tse tung, was becoming less revered and his doctrines questioned. After his death in 1976, the country went into turmoil, and the ideals of his Great Cultural Revolution didn't seem so great.

The decision to burn hundreds of historic paintings and artifacts, in the name of communism, was now regrettable, while capitalism looked good. Making money was gaining appeal while China as a tourist destination had lucrative possibilities.

**My travel diary begins:** This journal will contain random notes on our trip from Hong Kong to China, October 10-20, 1979. Charlie and I signed up for the tour through the China Travel Service. The country had been "opened up" to tourists for just a couple of years. The only way one could travel there was on a group visa, through China Travel Service. We had signed up five months ahead and were put on several waiting lists, so these tours were very popular. Parts of this journal's entries were written after returning home, or at the end of the trip, so the chronology may jump around.

**Entered prior to our departure:** Very popular indeed. Not only expatriates from Hong Kong, but fancy travel agencies in the United States had clients on waiting lists, hankering to see the PRC. Such travelers paid top dollar for luxury cruises from San Francisco to Singapore and Hong Kong. After a week's pampering of five-star living, the travelers would reach the final leg of the journey, under the auspices of China Travel Service. This experience was anything but luxurious, as the absence of amenities would be a big surprise. Hotel rooms lacking shampoo and lotions. Watery coffee. Pieces of hard candy the standard of complimentary refreshments. But despite the hardship, China had become a much sought-after tourist destination.

**Two days before our trip was to begin**: Mr. Wong, the China Travel Service agent in Hong Kong, called our apartment asking to speak to Mr. Charles Lee. Since Charlie was at the office, I took the message: Would Mr. Lee be willing to be the visa holder for the trip to Canton? He will only need to carry the documents and tourist papers on the train, then deliver them to the representative meeting your train in Canton.

"That would be fine," I told him. "Why did you choose my husband to do this?" I asked.

"Because he has a nice face on his passport picture," he replied.

Our group gathered on the platform at the Kowloon Railway Station, a 1920's brick building with an iconic clock tower, one of Hong Kong's few historic structures that hadn't been demolished for a modern replacement. Mr. Wong, the China Travel agent I had spoken to previously, greeted our group.

"You must be Mr. Lee," he said, recognizing Charlie from his photograph. He handed him a large manila envelope holding personal information, passports, and travel documents for the passengers on the trip. "Please give this to our agent who will be meeting you at the Canton railway station," he added.

Shepherding the group of forty-two travelers onto the train car, Mr. Wong then doled out red badges stating our names. Charlie's badge, as visa deliverer, was blue. Surreptitiously and shyly, we eyed each other, registering the people we'd be with for the next ten days. We were traveling with American friends from Hong Kong, George and Dinah Hutchinson, whom we knew through our sons who went to school together. I was excited about this trip. I loved trains, loved getting away, and was ready for a change. Chris and John were home with our amah Ah Fung, while parents of their friends would help carpool and arrange activities. We left the station precisely at noon on the "Kowloon and Canton Railway," with Mr. Wong waving goodbye from the platform.

**October 10:** The train is modern, comfortable, and smooth. White lace doilies are draped over the headrests. A pretty, young woman with short braids and an olive green cap is our conductor. Wearing a soldier-like Mao uniform, she greets us in the aisle. Her English is good and her expression eager. She hands out hard candy. There is a TV at the front of our car running tapes of Chinese acrobats.

The scenery is pastoral and beautiful between Hong Kong and Canton (our Travel Service agent says 'Canton,' but the name is in transition: Guangzhou? Kwangchow?) The farmland is vast, with tidy strips of different shades of green. We see casual water buffalo, and *Hakka* women in wide straw hats, bent over as they harvest the crops. Some carry bamboo poles with water buckets across their shoulders. No roads, just farms. We buy green tea on the train (it is not complimentary), only the tea leaves don't sink, so it's hard to drink. We and our fellow tour members look at each other and wonder how to manage the thick layer of soggy leaves. Use our teeth as strainers? We smile and shrug.

The train ride is four hours. The appointed group leader, my husband, moves us through customs. As of now he's unsuspecting of his role, assuming it's a one-time effort, only to find out later it has significant responsibility. We would discover that he was THE man for every transfer. We did not have an appointed guide who'd stay with us the entire trip. Like a baton in a relay, each city guide would send us off to the next destination and a new attendant, Charlie being the document bearer. And sometimes hotel room assigner. We are divided into two groups. We and the Hutchinsons are the only ones from Hong Kong. The rest are from the United States. We are in Group One.

The next China Travel man meets us at the Canton train station, and we board a bus as comfortable as a school bus. Straight-backed hard seats. Everything runs efficiently. We are staying at the White Cloud Hotel, about 10 minutes out of the city. Very modern, we are told.

The hotel was built in 1976. Thirty stories high, the rooms are bare except for the basic two beds, chair, table, etc. No rugs, just a beige vinyl floor. Somewhat like a hospital room. The 1950's style furniture is blond. The room is provided with a thermos of hot water and a tin of tea. On the thermos is a picture of apple blossoms. We dine at 6:30 in the tour group dining room. Dinner is good, although we are tired and hungry, so that's no measure of 'good.' It is much like college cafeteria food, creamed chicken and rice, but still it is good. Western cuisine is becoming a learning experience for the Mainland Chinese. There's a separate China Travel tour here as well on the other side of the room, all Americans. All wearing red badges.

After dinner, we take a taxi with our friends to Shamian, an island where foreign traders – mostly British and French – used to live and work, back in the opium days of the 1870's. We find Victorian buildings, some former embassies, on a street lined with banyan trees. The trees are dry and broken and in need of care and pruning. The mansions are run-down and falling apart. Locals live in them, squatter style, or else they are offices. Laundry hangs everywhere. The church has been turned into a printing facility.

**2019 (on the internet):** I find current pictures of Shamian showing precise architectural restoration to the foreign embassies. The church, Our Lady of Lourdes, has been restored to its original Gothic style with tall arched windows and cream-colored stucco. No longer in Mao outfits, but stylish jeans and Gap or Banana Republic sweatshirts, citizens stroll the riverside promenade now landscaped with healthy trees and tubs of colorful flowers.

**Oct. 11, Thursday:** Luggage out the door at 7:00 am. Breakfast at 7:30. We opt for dim sum. Looks better than the Western breakfast of runny fried eggs. (Charlie and I are familiar with the steamed pastries, a Chinese breakfast staple.) On the bus at 8:30. Off to 1.) A Buddhist temple; 2.) An arts and crafts factory; 3.) Foshan for lunch; 4) Drive to Canton airport for the flight to Hangchow. A busy day.

The arts and crafts factory, the first of several on the itinerary, is where they make Chinese paper-cuts – it's a room full of workers hand-cutting designs with small scissors. It looks like a class of kindergarten children cutting out valentines. Only here the cutters are elder craftspeople. The designs, intricate and complicated, involving multi-layers of paper forming dragons, peonies, and plum blossoms, are used in framed wall decorations. Seated at the other end of the large workroom, at a long table, are men and women painting ceramic Santa Clauses. Focused on their task, everyone silent. Celadon pottery with a greenish glaze is created; paper and silk lanterns, vases, and hand-painted silk paintings are in a separate area. We are urged by our guide to buy the wares, but we from Hong Kong are familiar with these goods. They are sold locally at China Products, a new shop promoting foreign trade. And the prices are cheaper in Hong Kong.

Next stop of the day is Foshan, a pretty town near Canton with shade trees and a factory where blue and white ceramic pottery is made. We eat on the 3rd floor of a rustic-looking restaurant. Here lunch is Chinese and delicious, not the attempt at Western cuisine that some establishments strive for. The first two floors of the wooden building are men only, eating at lacquered tables in the style of the Ming Dynasty. Here there are spittoons, trash on the floor, dirty dishes on the tables; although disgusting, it's unique. Cigarette smoke everywhere. The 3rd floor, for foreign tour groups, is clean and attractive with brightly polished dark wood floors and large windows that bring in daylight. After lunch we walk around a pretty neighborhood with wide, tree-lined streets. Curious school children surround us, coming to stare at the tall white people. Their teacher stands to the side. Then the bus to the airport.

**China Airlines from Canton to Hangchow.** Tomorrow we go to Shanghai. Chinese tea and hard candies are served on the plane. One hour flight. Arrive at Hangchow about 6:00 pm. Get on a lovely new bus with soft reclining seats, unlike the school bus-style one in Canton. Go to the Hangchow Hotel, have dinner, and I'm asleep at 8:30. A tiring day.

The Hangchow Hotel is wonderful. Big, spacious, 1930's type rooms. Space and sun everywhere. As described in our guidebook: "The Hangchow Hotel is a luxurious accommodation by PRC standards." It has high ceilings, verandas, and gardens. And it has giant overstuffed chairs with doilies. Good food. We've all switched to Western breakfasts at this point, as they have improved. Hangchow has lovely streets lined with oak trees. We are told Chairman Mao liked trees. Crowds collect around us everywhere. Charlie and George, both tall, stand outside the Friendship Store, as though celebrities. Some eager souls want to practice their English. Our guides keep taking us shopping. A Friendship Store is in every city. They sell Western-type clothing, an attempt at being modern. This one window has a mannequin wearing some baggy plaid skirt, and a pair of knee-high stockings on the legs, the kind of stockings to wear only with pants. The elastic top of them is in full view, calf-height, as though a style highlight. Only foreigners can shop in Friendship Stores, which seems odd. Local Chinese aren't allowed. But Western-style fashions are making an appearance on the locals. I can see the shift is coming, as more citizens are wearing navy blue cotton jackets, similar to smocks an artist would wear, rather than Mao outfits.

We go to the Leaning Pagoda. Lots of stairs to climb. Have a pleasant boat ride on West Lake, the pride of Hangchow. A great big lake and big shade trees, except for the pagodas and tea houses here and there. We go to a tea brigade, - a communist-run tea plantation. We get a brief introduction from the head comrade – a pretty lady who tells us how miserable the conditions were before the liberation and how wonderful everything is now. Chairman Mao made it all good. She beams with pride. We see beautiful, plump tea bushes rounded with precision, like sculpted hedges. The electric leaf-drying tubs remind me of old-fashioned washing machines. On our final day we go to a silk factory; the giant weaving machines are mesmerizing. I buy a gold brocade bureau scarf with whooping cranes. Then to a garden with goldfish and carp. (We've seen goldfish and carp everywhere), and then to the train station for our trip to Shanghai.

The Hangchow station is filled with more 1930's overstuffed armchairs and crocheted doilies on the headrests, the Chinese standard of luxury. On the train we are in a 4-person banquette with the Hutchinsons. Lace curtains are on the window. Tea is served. Later we have an elegant 5-course dinner in the gleaming white dining car, reminiscent of the Pullman days in America. We reach Shanghai at 9:00 pm.

We are staying at the Shanghai Mansions Hotel, a structure from the 1930's, the architecture similar to the pre-war New York apartment buildings on Park Avenue. We find out we will be in Shanghai one day longer than planned and Peking one day shorter. Everyone grouses and complains. Not unusual with China Travel. Our room is on the 2nd floor and is reasonably revolting. We are situated on the Bund, a road alongside the harbor. We face the canal, so there are horrible harbor smells, which actually disappear after a while. The people assigned (by Charlie) to the top floor rooms get beautiful renovated ones, but we didn't. Apparently it was luck of the draw, and we lucked out. Ours reminds me of one of Charlie's college apartments. The bathtub is gray with permanent dirt. A comb and brush have been graciously put out for us, with someone's hair in them. I don't know if it was meant as a hotel amenity or forgotten by the previous traveler.

This is where Charlie's role as visa-bearer gets stressful. Our fellow travelers had been presuming all along that he's a paid staff member for China Travel and they are angry. The local Shanghai guide hands him the task of assigning hotel rooms for the group. There aren't enough rooms, and it's assumed, by the hotel staff, that the two single women, strangers to each other, could share. This, of course, is met with outrage, and another single room is procured. Charlie is also requested to plan the itinerary for the following day. He selects a river trip (a particular interest for him), a visit to an exhibition hall, and a park. Meanwhile our companions complain to him the heat doesn't work in the hotel. Where is the real China Travel guide? Eventually the group processes that Charlie is just a sucker stuck with this job. Camaraderie builds. They appreciate his efficiency and good humor. Everyone relaxes and friendships build. We laugh a lot on the bus rides.

The first night in Shanghai he goes to bed with a double bourbon. Only the ice tastes terrible, which ruins it. At least bourbon is available, as is Scotch and brandy (a Chinese favorite).

After a night's sleep and breakfast, the group feels resigned about our itinerary mix-up, with the extra night in Shanghai. We have two wonderful groups – from Australia, Argentina, Hong Kong, Honolulu, and other US cities. All ages. One Chinese-American woman from San Francisco is able to locate the large western house she grew up in, her father being a banker who left the city in a hurry before Mao took over. It struck her with powerful emotions that she shared.

Our first morning in Shanghai we do general tour-bus sightseeing. The residential areas are significantly Western, left over from the booming days before liberation. There are many grand houses once belonging to traders and businessmen; the houses are now dirty and turned into factories or public housing. More lovely tree-lined streets. We go to an industrial exhibit in a mighty communist-style exhibition hall. We look at knitwear machinery and handicrafts. I purchase a hanging scroll magnificently written with fluid calligraphy. The text is the writing of a classical Chinese poet. I forget who.

The people here do not have that fresh country look as those in Hangchow. In Hangchow, the girls had cute short braids. In Shanghai they are making a sad stab at Western style. They wear the same baggy Mao pants, but some shapeless jacket or blouse on top. Many have "hair-dos," bouffant styles from the 60's. Probably copied from outdated American fashion magazines. Some of the shop windows display 60's-style dresses and skirts, although I have yet to see a woman in a skirt. There are people everywhere, and we collect crowds easily. They come out to study the foreigners. Early one morning, Charlie goes jogging through the streets and soon a clump of young men are running with him, practicing English.

After lunch we go to the Yu Yuan Garden and then the Jade Buddha temple. The Yu Yuan Garden has a small lake with a zig-zag bridge, crowded with local people in blue cotton jackets. The Jade Temple is empty, as it is only open to foreigners; Chinese citizens are not permitted. There is, in fact, a Buddha made of white jade. After dinner we walk over to the requisite Friendship Store. It's not crowded, so shopping is pleasant. We buy Mao hats for our sons and our nephews.

**Monday morning, Oct. 16:** A boat trip is scheduled on the Huangpu River. We see harbor sights, cargo ships, and naval vessels, from all over the world. Shanghai has a huge harbor. After lunch, The Children's Palace. This for me is a highlight. A former 1930's Gothic mansion turned into a school, it is for extra-curricular activities for gifted children, as well as outdoor sports for all children. The outdoor sports are really army training tactics for kids: scaling walls, crawling under nylon netting, etc. Little kids wearing khaki shirts and red neckties. Resembles a boot camp for soldiers. The artistic part is impressive. An orchestra of children play "Home on the Range." One 4-year-old boy plays the violin perfectly. No smiles, but a genius. Adorable. The headmistress of this school has a broad, proud smile. On the way to the school we stop to shop at two more Friendship Stores.

After dinner we go to a ballet. This turns out to be a Western Classical Variety Show. First, a wonderful maestro conducts the Shanghai Symphony with such choices as "The Blue Danube Waltz" and "Stars and Stripes Forever." He is like a Chinese Arthur Fiedler. The audience talks through it all. Then we watch some ballet skits. Every time a dancer fumbles, the audience laughs. The whole evening proves to be a remarkable study of the Chinese audience and the strange rudeness thereof. You'd think we were watching a baseball game.

**Oct. 17:** our last morning in Shanghai. We go to the Arts and Crafts Institute, which is another mansion. The old house fascinates me, European style, from another era. There are little crafts going on in every room. Paper cuts, ivory carving, needlepoint, lantern making. There is a needlepoint portrait of Chou En Lai on the wall (Premier of China, 1949-76). Ivory carvings of Marx and Lenin as well.

Late morning we fly to Peking. China Airlines and more hard candies and tea. Lunch in the Peking Airport. We go to the Temple of Heaven in a light rain. Beautiful. We are staying at the Friendship Hotel, which is 40 minutes out of the city. A disappointment as it is so far away, but we are lucky to be anywhere. Overbooking is a constant problem. Our original itinerary said we'd be in the Peking Hotel, the only Western hotel in Peking. There are so many tours going through now that some tours have been bumped out of Peking altogether. The Friendship Hotel looks good after the Shanghai Mansions. Clean bathroom, comfy beds with heavy quilts filled with cotton batting. The decor is bland, as it has been before. Two stark beds, a bureau, and the thermos of hot water, decorated with pink apple blossoms. A bare vinyl floor.

My journal ends here abruptly. I never finished the "Peking" part or the trip home. But I have the faded photographs of Tien An Men Square, Temple of Heaven, Imperial Palace, Ming Tombs, and a train trip to The Great Wall. All that in two days. And finally, the "Peking/Beijing" Airport, a rectangular yellow brick building with an industrial look.

Looking back 40 years to the Peking we knew, I remember a colorless city without a downtown, but instead, a spread of wide boulevards and few cars. Gray municipal buildings, massive and low, were prevalent, but spaced apart, giving the landscape a desolate look. Hundreds of people on bicycles swarmed the avenues, the main form of transportation. The most notable of automobiles were Buicks and Cadillacs, driven by chauffeurs for people of importance. Traffic lights were few - leaning on the horn being the standard method of navigation. Our bus driver honked continuously to get through the bicycle traffic jams, like a car trying to push its way through a cattle crossing. There were few tourists, and we with the China Travel Service tour had the Great Wall to ourselves.

Living in Hong Kong those years gave us the opportunity to travel throughout Asia. Besides China, we visited Singapore, the Philippines, Thailand, Malaysia, and farther afield. Sometimes Charlie and I traveled together, sometimes with Chris and John. The China trip was especially interesting, to witness a country on the cusp of becoming a major world power. Historically, it was a fascinating time.

I can get mired in nostalgia thinking of "times gone by." It was a vibrant stage of life for a young family. Sons in middle school, us in our thirties, and an energy we didn't know we had.

*Which way to the shrine?*

# 8

# A Shinto Shrine, 1989

CHARLIE AND I STOOD below the cherry trees and argued on a Saturday in March, in the early afternoon. With my back to the breeze, I held out the unfolded city map of Tokyo. It flapped a bit, and we tried to find the location of a restaurant recommended in the guidebook. According to this book, the restaurant was somewhere near the cemetery in which we stood. My L.L.Bean tote bag rested on the ground. It contained another guidebook, a subway map of Tokyo, and a directory of useful Japanese phrases. We were not tourists, my husband and I, but expatriates. We had been living in Tokyo for six weeks.

"Let's get on with this business of eating. I need food," I said.

To which Charlie said, "I'd rather go home and have a peanut butter sandwich. It's a lot easier, and cheaper."

"That's not the point. We're having this nice Japanese culture day, in case you hadn't noticed." The sarcasm felt good. Besides, I knew if he went home he'd spend the rest of the day watching CNN. All week long he worked hard, trying to grasp the subtleties of his Japanese office, the Tokyo branch of a New York investment firm. It was up to me to put together our weekend diversions.

This Saturday outing had gone well, so far. We'd visited the Edo part of the city, where the original township of Tokyo had been established. The walking tour from the guidebook included a Shinto shrine, an Edo-period calligraphy supply shop (still in business after 300 years), and a folk art museum. We skipped the museum, couldn't find the calligraphers', and enjoyed the quiet grounds of the shrine. We walked a lot for one morning; it was way past lunchtime.

Now we were embroiled in the classic arguments which stem from weariness and hunger and are usually fueled by things quite small. It was not just to do with being lost in this charming, confusing neighborhood that made us irritable. It was the disorientation in our lives. The comforting pattern of the day-to-day had yet to be developed. Ordinary things, such as food shopping and eating out, involved a huge amount of effort. I didn't even know how to buy rice: so many kinds in big plastic bags, with writing I couldn't read. I missed Uncle Ben's with the directions on the box. The currency confused me – I was never sure which bill to pull from my wallet. The numbers seemed enormous. A ten thousand yen note would cover an average trip to the supermarket. Because the doctrine of my Yankee upbringing taught me not to complain, I went about my days, cheerful enough. But standing in that cemetery filled with cherry trees, I weakened. I hadn't felt this homesick since I went away to camp in the third grade.

For lunch, the guidebook suggested a noodle restaurant that had been run by an esteemed samurai family for several generations. The book had an image of the Japanese characters – three single snowflake forms of *kanji* printed beside the phonetic spelling of the restaurant's name. We couldn't find it. Holding the page next to the *noren* (a hanging panel of fabric stating restaurant names), we could not find an exact match to the characters in the guidebook. Being illiterate gave me a sense of panic. But I was determined to finish this Saturday outing with an authentic Japanese meal. All over Tokyo the cherry trees had blossomed, but the day was windy, and erratic gusts blew petals about. Charlie and I stood arguing on ground that looked like pink snow.

The sandwich idea at home was tempting, but cowardly. It took courage to walk into an ethnic restaurant while heads turned and conversation stopped. It happened all the time, particularly in the historic districts of Tokyo. In my Japanese language lessons, I had so far only mastered my address. I hadn't advanced to "eating out" in Chapter 3, with the sketch of the smiling waiter. In fact, I always imagined the staff drawing straws to determine who'd wait on us, the Americans. Although English was a requirement in high school, the teachers were mostly native Japanese speakers, and their spoken words were hard to understand. Thus they were embarrassed to converse. And for us, it was humiliating to be handed a menu we couldn't read. Fortunately, the window displays always had plastic food models that were highlights of the menu, so we could always go outdoors and point. I mostly ordered tempura soba, a safe bet.

We finally gave up trying to find that one restaurant and decided to settle for a substitute. I had imagined a quiet place with dark, polished walls and waitresses padding about silently in *kimonos*. Leaving the grounds of the shrine, we walked in the direction of the subway. Occasionally we'd peer through the opening of the *noren*, but I felt conspicuous. Nothing seemed right. I was angry at my husband for never caring about food, the way I did. I was angry at the Japanese for creating such a confusing city. The streets not only meander, but they have no street names. Only the neighborhoods, with specific boundaries, were named. The house numbers made no sense to us. I was always lost. The citizens got lost as well.

Brooding, I dragged behind my husband through a residential area with small modern houses and laundry hanging in every yard. An old man was pruning one of several miniature bonsai trees he had along his front stoop. We exchanged hearty *kon-ni-chi-was* ("hello," the first word in Chapter One). Soon we got to a busy avenue, and could see in the distance the large surroundings of Ueno Station, where many subway and train lines connect. Also visible along the avenue, a line of fast food restaurants.

"McDonald's, great, let's go," he said.

I stayed sullen. Even in America I never went to McDonald's. I have my standards. But in Japan, on a day with scattering cherry blossoms? What a thought. On the other hand, there were the Golden Arches, and we were hungry.

As we went through the doors, a young woman in a McDonald's uniform and little cap was standing to the right. She said in Japanese the words meaning: "Welcome, please come in." Then, bending from the waist, she bowed. Escorting us to the food counters, she indicated, with her white-gloved hand, the shortest line. When she felt confident that we'd be all right on our own, she bowed again and returned to her place by the door.

The testy mood I'd arrived with quickly slid away. Of course I could not read the menu but the bright, color photographs of Big Macs and French fries were universally understandable. I could communicate.

The restaurant was busy; we ate upstairs. Two older women wearing the housewife style of cotton kimono – a custom disappearing with the grandmother generation – were eating at the table next to ours. One had on rhinestone-rimmed glasses, and they both had dyed hair the color of black shoe polish. Chatting at a fast pace, they finished up their coffee and cardboard-boxed apple pies. Apparently deciding to go downstairs for more coffee, they stood up. Then they took some coins from their purses and left the wallets, fat with credit cards and yen, on top of their empty table, to keep their places reserved. Together, my husband and I stared at these unattended wallets, left behind in total trust, with awe. Stealing, to the Japanese, is something that happens only in other countries. This was as culturally significant as a Shinto shrine. Mid-chatter, they bowed quick little bows to us to apologize for squeezing through our close-together tables, saying, *Sumimasen* (excuse me). In time, the women returned with their coffee, bowed, and apologized again as they slid between the tables and continued with their conversation.

We ate in silence for a while.

"Maybe after lunch we could look for that folk art museum," Charlie said.

Happy with this suggestion, I nodded, and finished the last of my French fries.

Pulling the map from my bag, I unfolded it across the table. We pinpointed the station, this McDonald's, and the short walk to the museum. The women next to us got involved, and in Japanese and hand gestures, showed us the best walking route to take. I also pinpointed a specific sensation that rippled through me. At that moment, I started my friendship with Japan.

---

*This essay was first published in an anthology titled, "They Only Laughed Later, Tales of Women on the Move," in 1997. Modified, 2019.*

*Charlie at the helm of "Camilla."*

# 9

## WAKING UP IN CUTTYHUNK

WHAT WE HAVE HERE are two forward berths, two portholes, an overhead hatch with a round window. My berth is the one on the left – the port side. It is 6:15 in the morning, and I am in it – my bed – looking up through the skylight, trying to read the weather. Yesterday it rained. Last night there was a thunderstorm, then a cool, damp breeze came through. What I see is an all-over gray. But a bright gray, more silver than slate.

If there's one thing I can do, it's sleep on a boat. It's the gentle rocking, the scent of ocean, and the muffled rhythm of ripples as they slap on the hull. Ours is a wooden boat, so the sound is especially dull and lulling, unlike the echoing ping of waves against fiberglass. We are tied to a 300-pound concrete mooring at the bottom of the harbor which makes us secure – both me and the boat. If we'd used our own anchor, there's always a chance of dragging on the soft sand and possibly hitting another boat in the middle of the night. Not that I worry about drifting. Charlie is an excellent sailor. At sea he is knowledgeable and cautious. He sleeps lightly, with a subconscious ear out for stronger winds or sudden squalls – much like a mother's ear for her children. While cocooned in my berth, I sleep heavily, and I hardly dream. But I haven't always felt this calm; it has taken me forty-four years of marriage to come to terms with cruising. It took some self-counseling, tough-love, and compromising.

I was born between two generations of philosophy. The first being, keep your feelings to yourself. Don't bring up anything unpleasant or of a prickly nature. Let your thoughts fester and multiply. The generation thereafter discovered that confrontation works better. Be direct, say how you feel, get it off your chest. Although against my upbringing, I recently made the transition. I managed to announce that I, well, don't really like boats all that much. I was partially successful.

I was not yet familiar with the word "denial," in the context of how it is used today. A word I kept hearing in regard to relationships, and it began to sink in, how it applied to ours. Denial to process how one's wife doesn't take to the open sea. That is when my tough-love kicked in: I hadn't been firm enough. Read my lips: I don't want to go out on the boat for ten days. I miss my shower. I'd rather flush a toilet than pump out a head. I don't like going out on the ocean in our small boat, to roll and surge in fifteen knot winds. I will never in my wildest dreams want to take our boat up the Hudson River and down the St. Lawrence Seaway. These are the things my husband talks of. He dreams of retirement, of going cruising for months at a time, with me, his favorite companion, as first mate. Throughout his outlandish spoken daydreams, my jaw would tighten while I'd remain silent. That was then.

After numerous years, I came up with a compromise. Charlie goes cruising with his boating pals. Friends he's known forever. Good weather or foul, they go out. They play with the electronic navigation system, tinker with the bilge pump, talk about diesel engines. They'll heat up a can of Dinty Moore beef stew while steering the boat over four-foot swells. In the narrow berths they sleep, two grown men in sleeping bags, snoring. For my nautically obsessive husband, the intensity of his cruising desire aboard his beloved *Camilla* is satisfied. Yes, he named the boat after me. I would have preferred something like Osprey or Loon, but didn't have the heart to tell him back then. I didn't speak up. But what I do love is staying put in a harbor. What I like is being able to see land, row ashore, go on walks. I want to hear the birds. That's how it is now.

My mind begins to map out the day. A trip ashore after breakfast and a walk before getting underway. I need to walk. Skyward from my berth, I watch the gray dissipate into sunshine. The hatch is propped open with a soggy volume of *Moby Dick*, letting in just enough air to move through the cabin, clearing out the moisture from the night before. There's revving of an outboard motor nearby, probably someone taking a dog to the beach for its morning run. The enticing aroma of coffee wafts from the galley as Charlie pours boiling water through a filter into a thermal carafe. In a minute he'll bring me a mug of it, black, which I'll set on the little shelf by my berth, pushing aside a book, my earrings, and my watch. I had hoped to get through Herman Melville's classic, but, once again, it didn't work out. Instead I'm absorbed in a fat novel by Ken Follett, where the action takes place in the Middle Ages. The story's engrossing; I am speeding through it. But how delicious this is, not just the coffee, but being able to read in bed. In the galley, Charlie rattles around, getting out Cheerios, cereal bowls, blueberries, milk. He'll wipe off the deck chairs with a towel and we'll have breakfast outside. On the boat I am a princess.

This is the last day of our five-night cruise. The weather has been perfect; some rain at night but mostly sun and not much wind. Later this morning we'll head back to Padanaram Harbor in South Dartmouth, where I embarked. There we'll have lunch on board and admire the magnificent sailboats moored in the harbor. Our friend, Maynard, will meet us with my car; we'll change places. I'll drive an hour and fifteen minutes back to Narragansett, and he and Charlie will battle the terrifying (to me) racing currents through Wood's Hole, loving every minute of the excitement. The car logistics work. Much of cruising is about logistics, which to enthusiasts is part of the fun.

Half-way through my coffee, I pull myself up to look out the porthole, which is about eye level when I sit up straight in the bunk. I see a stretch of narrow beach with a line of dark seaweed left by the receding tide. Last night when I went to bed, the scene from the porthole was the Cuttyhunk pier, surrounded by lobster boats and multiple dinghies tied to floats. Now what I'm looking at is the beach. During the night, all the boats had gently swung on their moorings as the wind changed direction. This different view from the window surprises me for a moment, and I wonder where the dock went…then I remember. The nuance of the wind shift confused my orientation.

We are situated at the outer edge of the mooring field, away from the dock and nearer the scruffy beach on the opposite side of the harbor. The "field" consists of about seventy-five moorings placed in a grid pattern, like dots on a piece of graph paper. The moorings belong to the Town of Gosnold, hardly a town, but they call it that on Cuttyhunk Island. There is an ice cream store on the wharf and a shed that sells shellfish from a local oyster farm. Up the hill from the harbor is a small grocery store. There are no restaurants. Cuttyhunk is the southernmost island at the end of the Elizabeth Island chain that starts at Woods Hole. An Englishman named Bartholomew Gosnold named the chain of islands, developed for farming, in 1602. We are here on a busy July weekend. Every mooring is taken. In the evening the harbormaster will come alongside each boat and collect the mooring rental fee, forty dollars a night.

Because of our proximity to the beach, we are surrounded by dog people. There are old dogs with old people, dogs who are too ornery to be left in a kennel, or owners too doting to leave them behind. In the early light of morning, the people bring their dogs to the beach, where they scurry around and do their business. Anticipation and happiness shine on their furry faces as they approach the land, poised like figureheads on bowsprits. Wagging and wagging, they wait eagerly until they're able to leap ashore and run freely on the beach. I can relate to their need for space.

On one side of us is a beautiful sloop with a dark blue hull, elegant lines, and an elderly Golden Retriever sitting on the deck. The boat is quite big, maybe forty feet, and manned solely by a husband and wife who probably have had years of sailing experience together. Just the two of them. The dog's face is whitish, similar to the color of the man's hair. It is an effort for the couple to lower him into the bobbing, gray, inflatable dinghy. They carefully cradle him in their arms and settle him down.

Moored on our other side is a power boat, and another dog, a small, gray terrier, scampering and barking on deck. Also on board is a mom and a dad, two playful young girls, and a quiet teenage boy. The white fiberglass boat is maybe thirty-five feet long, not very big for a family of five with a yapping dog to spend a weekend aboard. It is the kind of boat you'd see at a boat show, very efficient and clean, easy to maintain. Last evening, the girls were like otters as they slipped in and out of the water, jumping from the swimming platform, frolicking in a big inflatable tube. They have identical blond hair and are close in age, maybe seven and nine. The dad towed the rubber tube from behind his dinghy and pulled the girls around the harbor, while mom paddled off on her own in a red kayak. When the four of them were away from the boat, the teenage boy sat on the swimming platform and smoked.

*Camilla* is a 31-foot power boat, which resembles a lobster boat, or more accurately, a Northwest troller from Vancouver, Canada. She was designed by an esteemed naval architect of fishing boats named William Garden. "She's a beauty!" other boaters call to us. "Prettiest boat in the harbor." They come alongside in their dinghies, nosing around the hull, asking questions. "Where was she built?" "How big is the engine?" Charlie beams while trying to stifle his blatant pride. The conversations can get detailed and lengthy.

Boats and cruising, I believe, are a part of a person's genes. My husband grew up in a nautical family and was sailing a fifteen-foot Beetle Cat by himself when he was eight years old. I am from a non-nautical family, although I spent my summers on the shore and am familiar with currents and tides. When I met my husband, at age 17, I knew nothing of boats. Part of my becoming smitten with him had to do with how skillful and agile he was at the helm. He'd push the tiller this way and that, the sail would fill or luff. Coming about, hard alee. We'd jibe or head up into the wind and go nowhere. Although I was filled with admiration, I was always happy to head back to shore.

It was after we got married (I was 21) when I became un-smitten with boating. But I'm good now. In August we'll go to Nantucket to visit his sister, Mags. Charlie and a friend will take our boat over from Wickford. If the weather is favorable, they'll be happy. If the seas are rough, they'll pound the swells and embrace the adventure. As for me, I will drive from Narragansett to Hyannis where I can leave my car at a parking lot, then step aboard the fast ferry for a one-hour trip across Nantucket Sound. On the island, Charlie will meet me at Nantucket's bustling port at the center of town. Intricate logistics fall into place involving moorings and launches and passing my car keys to the boating friend, who will then backtrack my journey to Narragansett. In Nantucket we'll spend two or three nights, depending on our mood, anchored away from the busy harbor in a quieter cove. During the day with crowds of tourists, we'll stroll around town on the cobblestone streets, poking in shops, and standing in line for an overpriced ice cream cone. We'll have lunch with his sister Mags and other friends. The best part of cruising.

At the end of the day, Charlie will rev up the outboard of our dinghy, and we'll putter back, away from the crowds, to *Camilla*. Dinner will be on board: pasta, salad, and cookies from a local bakery. From our proximity to the beach I'll listen to birds, the slight lap of waves, and watch the dog owners ferry their pets ashore. And I'll sleep soundly with the cradling motion of *Camilla*.

(*Written in 2008.*)

*Day six, the Grand Tetons.*

# 10

## WESTWARD, HO

### ROAD SCHOLAR TOUR #20297

#### BLACK HILLS OF SOUTH DAKOTA AND
#### WYOMING'S YELLOWSTONE/TETON NATIONAL PARKS

**June 7 – June 15, 2015**

A BUSLOAD OF ELDERS TRAVELS on Route 90 from Rapid City, South Dakota to Jackson, Wyoming. I am on the bus. Motor coach, I should say. It is an 8-day tour of Yellowstone National Park and the Grand Tetons, arranged by a travel group called "Road Scholar." This is a first-time experience for me, traveling solo, without a friend. Being in a busload of senior citizens is not an image I want to dwell on. We wear badges that hang from the neck by a cord, stating our names and hometowns. For me, there's a stigma about all this as we embark and disembark at every tourist plaza to use the restrooms and stretch our legs. But hey, these are my demographic people. And we're not geezers.

The magnet for this trip is, of course, the iconic scenery of the West. I've never visited a national park and look forward to seeing bison and elk, Old Faithful, and big sky country. I want to see the grandeur of the Grand Tetons. In Rhode Island, I have the dramatic ocean. I get to watch the power of the surf crashing on the rocks every day. I don't take for granted how shifting tectonic plates brought this granite coastline from Africa. But now it's time to experience the mountains and a different part of the earth's crust. Besides, as a child, I had the View-Master reel of Yellowstone National Park and the picture of Old Faithful has stayed in my mind.

Traveling alone is part of this adventure. I wanted this. The Independent Widow. The Independent Widow makes it to the Howard Johnson

Express Inn at the Rapid City Airport. Lewis and Clark traveled this route.

**Day 1:** After we arrive in South Dakota, the shuttle takes me and a few others to the hotel. We gaze out the windows without speaking, for which I am grateful. It's been a long day of travel. I'm not ready for chitchat. Can't wait to get to my room and wash my face. A private bathroom with little wrapped-up soaps and white towels will feel as good as a five-star hotel.

My 3rd floor room looks over a rectangular, brick high school centered in a black asphalt parking lot. It is Sunday, no cars on the lot. Taking off my sneakers and socks, I collapse on the bed, so happy for solitude. I make myself a cup of coffee on the flimsy little coffee maker that's provided. I love these machines. I've mastered them all.

After a welcome but brief lie-down and some unpacking, I take the elevator down to the Ho Jo Hospitality Lounge at 6:00, per the schedule.

Our Road Scholar guides are Pat and Paul Barber, a Mr. and Mrs. team. The Mrs. – Pat – is standing by the refreshments. The pub-like lounge features a counter with big urns of coffee and juice and a column of soft drink dispensers. On the square tables around the room, baskets of pretzels and popcorn have been placed. Also on the counter is a jumbo box each of cabernet sauvignon and pinot grigio. I want the red wine so badly, I forget my manners and head there first.

"I'll bet you're Camilla from Rhode Island," Pat says, stopping me as she procures my hanging name badge from a box.

I am one of the last to arrive. The group has spread itself around the room, four seats to a table.

"May I join you?" I ask at a place with a man and a woman.

"Please do!"

We introduce ourselves, holding up our name badges for a visual reference. Ginger and Jim from Tennessee. So far, so good.

Pat Barber is sharp, engaging, and genuinely upbeat. Falling into our median age bracket, she has frosted blond hair that's short and well-cut, and a healthy demeanor. With mike in hand, she conducts the welcoming speech and orientation. She introduces Paul, her husband, who stands at her side. Lacking the animation of his wife, he takes over and offers more information on the days ahead. Tri-fold brochures are distributed containing the week's schedule. They are printed, single-spaced, on budget paper, and crammed with itinerary. Road Scholar is a no-frills tour company. We are going to be busy.

An evening walking tour of downtown Rapid City brings us to an old-fashioned Main Street, devoid of traffic and people. It is almost like a movie set. An abandoned granary, "Aby's Feed and Seed" in washed-out letters, stands at the edge of town. The city's pride is the "Walk of the Presidents." There's a life-size bronze cast of each United States President at every street corner, that (to me) seems quite bizarre. Richard Nixon, James Garfield. Bill Clinton with his saxophone. You never know who you'll bump into next. Most of the old store-fronts now seem to be either real estate offices or insurance firms. In the brochure, our schedule for the following day reads:

**Day 2:** *6:00 AM Self-serve breakfast opens. 7:30 Depart hotel for Mount Rushmore. 10:15 AM Depart Mt. Rushmore for Crazy Horse Monument. 12:30 PM depart Crazy Horse for Hot Springs, lunch at Woolly's. Visit "Mammoth Site" after lunch. 3:30 PM depart Mammoth Site for a drive through Custer State Park. 6:30 arrive back to hotel. Dinner at hotel. Overnight Rapid City, SD.*

Viewing the real Mt. Rushmore after only seeing it in photographs is like admiring Monet's "Water Lilies" at the Metropolitan Museum in New York; not just a print on a hospital wall. For me, there was a hint of kitsch with the faces of those four Presidents (Washington, Jefferson, Lincoln, and Teddy Roosevelt) carved in the side of a mountain. Something like having the face of Queen Elizabeth in bas-relief on a teapot.

A short bus ride takes us to Crazy Horse Monument. In the mountainside genre of Mt. Rushmore, Crazy Horse is still a work-in-progress and has been since 1948. The private funds have stopped and started since its inception. Crazy Horse, a member of the Lakota Tribe, was instrumental in keeping his tribe from being located to a reservation. At Crazy Horse I experience my first tourist gift shop. This one is large. Tourist shops are plentiful, but I never tire of combing through T-shirts, silver jewelry, turquoise, moccasins, bandannas, coffee mugs, and beaded belts. I am tempted by it all.

The next stop, the "Mammoth Site," is a surprise. I am moved by the story. In 1975 a builder began work on a development in Hot Springs, South Dakota. While excavating, the workers came upon strange looking bones. Then a large tusk. Findings revealed that 26,000 years ago it had been a watering hole popular with mammoths, woolly and other types. A sinkhole developed around the pond, it collapsed, and all the mammoths fell down the steep slopes into the water and drowned. It's a sad picture, a watering hole opening up and trapping all these species from the Ice Age, but how convenient for future study. What you get is a well-preserved variety-pack of mammoth relics.

The end of Day Two brings us back to a spaghetti and meatball dinner at the Ho Jo Hotel. This is not a trip of fine dining or fine wines, but the cabernet from a gallon-size box could have been from the wine cellar of Chef Jacques Pepin for all I cared.

**Day 3:** *6:00 AM Self-serve breakfast. 7:00 AM Bring your own suitcase to coach. 7:30 Depart for Wyoming. Travel the wide-open spaces of Eastern and Central Wyoming. Sack lunch in Sheridan. Afternoon: travel across the Bighorn Mountains and through beautiful Shell Canyon. 5:00 PM Arrive at The Cody Hotel.*

Wide open spaces indeed. Vast expanses of green grass and happy wild-life. The previous month brought abundant rain; bison and prong-horned antelope are foraging away. Prairie dogs, moose, horses, cattle. A couple of retreating black bears. Today is a long day in the motor coach, but the rest period is needed. I have hardly seen a man-made structure all day other than tastefully appointed comfort stations along the way, complete with tourist information and gift shops. The view from my bus window is expansive from its elevated vantage point. Our seats are assigned with name and hometown prominently displayed on the window. The labels are clear plastic and removable, the font substantial. Every morning, Pat and Paul, and our bus driver Corey, unpeel the labels and rotate the arrangement by one row clockwise. This offers a change of tour members across the aisle and helps us to remember names. Being alone, I always have an empty seat next to me. A first class luxury.

As a group we are loosening up. Pat conducts corny games on the coach, at which I roll my eyes. Then partake. "What's your state flower?" she asks. A few hands go up. She walks the aisle with a mike like a talk show host. My hand pops up: "I don't know my state flower, but I can tell you the state appetizer of Rhode Island. It's calamari." I get into talking about my son in the squid business, for all to hear, which leaps into a discussion about the fishing industry.

We are getting to know one another. Bob, a retired engineer, is a member of the American Pencil Collectors Society. He has 1,500 pencils. I've met two retired math teachers and one science teacher. We have a woman with a bad attitude and food allergies, who vocally picks apart most of her meals. I assumed I'd be traveling with a pack of widows, like myself, but it seems to be mostly couples. They walk in pairs, shoulders touching. At the end of the day, Bob gives me a pencil which has "for lefties only" printed on the side. To us lefties anything written on a pencil is upside-down and backwards. It's a treat to read it right-side up.

I doze, drifting back to the intensity of trip preparations. The notes to my house-sitter regarding dog, cat, trash day, and so on. The sorting of medication into my day-by-day pill container. What to pack.

The coach pulls into our hotel parking lot in Cody, Wyoming, home of Buffalo Bill. Downtown Cody is semi-Wild West and semi-restaurants-of-all-ethnicities. The itinerary states: "Dinner on Your Own." Here comes my first sense of aloneness. Thus far, we'd been herded along, not having to make a decision. Now I'm feeling pathetic. New friends from Connecticut ask me to join them. Phew. I am grateful for their kindness. We eat at a Japanese restaurant where I have soggy tempura.

**Day 4:** *Cody, Wyoming. 6:45 AM Place luggage outside your door. 7:45 Depart hotel for Buffalo Bill Center of the West in Cody. 11:00 AM Depart museum. Stop at Buffalo Bill Dam before entering Yellowstone Park. Sack lunch. Visit Mud Pots before arrival at Lake Cabins. 5:30 PM Walk to dinner anytime (use coupon) at Lodge Cafeteria. Stay far away from Bison!*

"The Buffalo Bill Center of the West," I'd imagined would be a rustic wooden building, housing life-sized dioramas of Indians roasting maize and families heading west in covered wagons. But no. The Center is a sophisticated art museum that could be dropped into any major city and fit in. Works by American artists such as Bierstadt and Remington filled the galleries. At the far end of the main gallery, a large window faces the hilly outdoors, and there is Buffalo Bill himself, on horseback, standing (in bronze) atop a hummock.

Also unexpected is a fine cafe in the museum's central lobby, where I have my first latte since Starbucks in the Chicago Airport. Wyoming doesn't seem to take coffee as seriously as we do on the East Coast. Alone, I sit at a prominently placed high-top table and savor the quality caffeine and the calming moment to observe my surroundings. Traveling solo still feels comfortable. Maybe I'm good at living inside my head. My Road Scholar companions, with whom I am lightly bonding, pass by and we exchange our sentiments on the trip so far. Some admire me for my "sense of self," a quality I never gave thought to. At the lower level of the Buffalo Bill Center I do, in fact, find a covered wagon fitted with pots and pans and a small cast iron stove. Emotion sweeps through me as I ponder the motivation and bravery of the American pioneer.

The forthcoming "sack lunch," listed on the day's itinerary, proves to be several coolers filled with sandwiches from a Subway that our tour guides snuck off to while we toured the museum. At a woodsy picnic area, Pat and Paul pass out the wrapped sandwiches. Each person happily makes a selection and takes it to a picnic table. Except the food-allergies lady. This unhappy woman has a hissy fit because the special meal she'd ordered didn't appear. "I told Road Scholar when I signed up that I can't have processed meat. And I have to have gluten-free bread!" she ranted. The rest of us who are waiting, stand back, embarrassed, looking down at the grass, while she lists her allergies. Her husband, a short man, stands silently aside. (I understand her frustration; this could be dangerous. Having friends with allergies, I realize it's hard. But she handles it badly.)

Carrying my Italian sub and a bottle of water, I sit at an empty table except for a pale couple from Illinois. He's a retired postal worker, she a school teacher. My new best friend Ruth Ann calls from a crowded table to sit with her, but I do what I feel is right. Branch out. The Illinois couple and I talk about geysers. Meanwhile, raucous laughter explodes from Ruth Ann's table, of which I am envious. This is like a high school cafeteria, when you're with the loser group.

Now the "mud pots." Here the motor coach pulls into a stop at a bizarre moon-like landscape filled with gurgling pools here and there that quietly erupt and steam and burp in a variety of colors. Geothermal activity at work. I learn what a *fumarole* is (a steam vent where hot sulphuric gases emerge). Wooden boardwalks carry us over the ground surface, giving us closer views of the Disneyesque scene: One can imagine gremlins chatting underneath the surface of the bubbling pools. A rotten-egg aroma permeates the air – a strange smell, but not unpleasant. Just one more reminder of the topography. I love this weirdness. Checking my worn-out itinerary, I take a look to see what comes next and am happy to read it's the overnight accommodations.

The nostalgic atmosphere of the Lake Lodge and Cabins in Yellowstone Park make up for the lack thereof at the Howard Johnson Motel in Rapid City. I have a cabin to myself. Built in the 1940s, these are rustic little structures, painted yellow, with knotty pine walls inside. The pine-needled paths bring to mind the camp I went to in Maine when I was 10. I am grateful to the U.S. Department of the Interior to only allow approved national park hotels, barring the customary chains. A Yellowstone Marriott or Holiday Inn would not be right. This is an adventure.

The Lake Lodge is a big, welcoming, white clapboard building with an ample high-ceilinged interior, a good bar, and a grand piano at which a young African-American man plays Gershwin and Cole Porter. Comfortable, oversized chairs are arranged in groupings. I don't know where to place myself for an after dinner wine. The bar, I decide. Almost every oversized lounge chair is occupied by a person thumbing an iPhone.

**Day 5.** *6:30 AM breakfast opens - Lake Hotel dining room. Use your coupon. 7:30 AM luggage INSIDE cabin for bellman. 8:30 AM departure. Travel the Lower Loop Road this morning to the Grand Canyon of the Yellowstone, Lower Falls, visitors center and watching for animals. Lunch at Canyon Complex. 5:30 PM arrive Old Faithful area. Overnight at Old Faithful Inn. Dinner is on your own.*

At the Yellowstone Lodge breakfast, I have a table by the window in a dining room filled with light and have the pleasure of ordering two fried eggs over-easy from a waitress. So far, the breakfasts have been "buffet style," lidded steam trays containing surprises. The day is a full motor coach journey with, among other things, mountains, wildflowers, waterfalls, prairie dogs, and a black bear or two to view.

Late afternoon the motor coach arrives at the Old Faithful Inn. The Inn is magnificently large and rustic, with natural woodwork and exposed beams offering appropriate ambiance for a wilderness lodge. I imagine myself as a woman in the displayed sepia photographs, wearing a long black skirt, white shirt, and straw boater hat. Fishing rod in hand. And yes, next to the lodge, is Old Faithful, just as it was on my 1950 View Master reel.

The geyser erupts every 90 minutes or so from a moonscape of colorless ground. A designated clock in the hotel lobby displays the timing of the next event. As from my memory of the pictures, a circle of onlookers surround it, as I am doing now. When Old Faithful is quiet, steam gurgles on the ground, going this way and that depending on the wind. Then whoosh, another forceful eruption, straight up 150 feet, plus or minus, up to the sky. How lucky am I to have a 2nd floor room facing the site, so I can read on my bed, wait for the next upsurge, and contemplate what power must be stirring so in the depths of the earth.

This is another "dinner on your own" night. Because the only option is the rustic hotel restaurant, it relieves the pressure of making a choice. Tired of the effort of being sociable, I sit in a quiet corner by the window and enjoy a comforting meal of grilled salmon.

**Day 6:** *6:30 AM breakfast. 6:45 luggage OUTSIDE door. 8:00 am departure. Travel the southern part of Yellowstone to Grand Teton National Park. 10:45 – 4:00 PM Travel Jenny Lake Loop to town of Jackson. Overnight in Jackson Lake Cottages. Yes, bellmen.*

Today the weather is warm and dry, the sky bright blue, the Grand Tetons snow-capped. Every day has been perfection. During the journey our motor coach pulls into a parking area so we can disembark and stare at the mountains with wonder. One of our tour mates, Tom, known as "the photographer," sets up his tripod and takes close-up pictures of wildflowers. I am standing in magnificence. Somewhere in these yellow-bells and larkspur, I lose my expensive prescription sunglasses.

Jackson Lake Lodge is one more tribute to our national parks. I sign up for a rafting tour down the Snake River after dinner (an extra expense). The moon is round, full, precise. On this rafting trip are non-Road Scholar travelers, and I'm glad to step out of the retiree demographic. I talk with a young woman and her two daughters on holiday from an Air Force Base in Colorado Springs. Her husband had just been deployed to Qatar for a year. Not combat duty. The river ride is perfect for me, no big splashes or bouncing through rapids, but still an adventure.

Suddenly I'm looking forward to going home; this always happens to me on trips. I have Day Seven and Day Eight ahead before returning to Rapid City. I wish I could stay another night at the Jackson Lake Lodge and have another breakfast looking at elk at the foot of the Grand Tetons. Those antlers. One night is not enough here. I would like time to hike the trail that meanders from the grounds of the inn and skip a visit somewhere else.

**Day 7:** *Depart Jackson Lake Lodge for Casper, WY. 4:00 – 5:00, National Historic Trails Interpretive Center. 5:15, Hampton Inn. Group Dinner.*

We've left the Grand Teton National Park and are back on the highway. I love the bus rides, with the high observation vista and reclining seats. Our experienced and balding bus driver Corey is as likable and important as our guides. Looking at my Wyoming map, I see how far we have been and how far we have to go.

The "National Historic Trails Interpretive Center," a large, new, sterile building, is a dud, with an empty parking lot large enough to hold many tour buses. The vintage sepia photographs interest me. One "hands-on" exhibit draws my attention: a replica of a covered wagon where you climb onto the seat, push a button and it simulates the rough ride a wagon would make over badly rutted and uneven trails. However, when I push the button, nothing happens. Members of the staff come, but still no luck. Disappointing.

I will be happy to reach the next stop, the solid and predictable

Hampton Inn, an entry back to reality. Paul gives detailed lectures en route. One about the coal industry in Wyoming as we drive past mining machinery and miles of freight cars. Many of us doze. As we leave Wyoming, he becomes animated talking about Sturgis, South Dakota, home of Harley Davidson motorcycles. This year (2015), in August, will be the 75th anniversary of the motorcycle rally. By popular demand (by some of us), we take an unscheduled side trip through downtown Sturgis, where everything is Harley. We will stop at a big Harley-everything store. I almost buy a tasteful belt with a small logo on it, but the price, it turns out, is $125.00. The town is expecting 10,000 bikers for the rally.

**Day 8:** *6:00 AM Self-serve breakfast. 7:10 AM Bring your luggage to coach. 7:30 Depart/Travel back to Rapid City via Devils Tower. Sack lunch after walk around Devils Tower. 5:30 Arrive at Howard Johnson Inn and Suites. No bellstaff. 6:30 PM catered dinner in hotel meeting room. Overnight Rapid City, SD.*

Here my energy is petering out; we reach the brown Devils Tower. Fifty million years ago molten magma, contracting and cooling, forced its way up, ending as this cone-shaped tower, 867 feet high. Although an important geological feature, it lacks intrigue after the grandeur of Yellowstone and the Grand Tetons. I'm tired and return to our motor coach ahead of time, before departure. Other travelers are on the bus as well, dozing.

The coach takes us back to our original starting place, the Howard Johnson Inn in Rapid City. This time my room is on a higher floor, looking at the familiar "Aby's Seed and Feed" which I find to be sentimental. Our farewell dinner, in the hotel meeting room, is lasagna and salad brought in from a local restaurant. We are encouraged to create skits and such. I write a poem in tribute to our guides and bus driver. Big applause. The best is after dinner, holding hands in a circle singing "God Bless America." You'd think things couldn't get any cornier, but I loved it. We were a genial group, but there it ended. My friend Ruth Ann and I exchange email addresses.

**Day 9:** *Self-serve style breakfast and independent departures. Noon hotel checkout. Thank you for coming, keep memories of this area in your heart and keep on traveling with Road Scholar!*

**"Bonus" Day 10:** *Sleep overnight on a cot in the American Airlines terminal at O'Hare International Airport in Chicago.*

The commuter plane takes off, but some freakish weather pattern coming from Texas, diverts us to Appleton, Wisconsin. There I have nachos and cabernet sauvignon. The co-pilot is in the bar with us (not drinking), excitedly showing the weather screen on his cell phone, which displays swirling circles of different colors. We do fly to Chicago, two hours late, and miss the flight to Providence. Then the airport shuts down, the erratic weather having returned. It becomes clear to me, at 8:15 pm, I will be spending the night at O'Hare.

"Where's the comfiest place to sleep?" I ask a United agent who is coming on duty.

"I believe they'll be setting cots up in the American terminal; it's closed for the night," he says.

I do a high-speed walk to American, following the overhead signs. Sure enough, stacks of cots are arriving in racks and are getting unfolded and set up in the empty terminal. I am lucky and get in on this at the start. I follow an older couple, meaning my age, and we stick together, hoping for preferred Senior Citizen treatment. This couple had just flown in from Austria and missed the short flight to their home in Wisconsin.

By now word has gotten out about cots in the American Airlines terminal, and people are arriving. There are 200 cots and 400 people. We are given blankets, pillows, and toothbrushes. Hard to sleep under the bright lights of Terminal C. I doze a bit, clutching my purse, listening to repetitive announcements: "This is a non-smoking terminal..." "Do not leave your bags unattended..." At 4:00 AM airport personnel walk through: "Rise and shine everyone!" We have to get up in order for the airport to start a new day. The metal gates of McDonald's, Starbucks, and Dunkin' Donuts are squeakily raised by the staff.

I get on a 6:00 AM flight to Boston, not Providence. My friend Ellie, God bless her, meets me at Logan and drives me to my car at T.F. Greene. My suitcase catches up with me the next day.

Weary and finally home, I shake out the contents of my carry-on tote onto my bed. Prominent are brochures from "The National Park Service, U.S. Dept. of the Interior." There's Yellowstone, Grand Tetons, Pony

Express, Devils Tower, Oregon Trail. The remembering fills my heart with passion for the American West and I start to hum, "This Land is My Land." My cat jumps up, stretches across the informative literature, and washes a paw.

I did it; I traveled alone. I am proud to be able take a trip without my husband, and he would be proud of me as well. But it's not a hardship to travel through Wyoming on a comfortable bus, be taken care of, and be immersed in the scenery of our magnificent national parks.

*Charlie, a free spirit.*

# 11

## THE AZORES, 2018

I'M IN THE AZORES on vacation. Specifically one island, São Miguel, but I like to throw out, "The Azores," which, in my mind, conjures a *National Geographic* cover. This is a holiday with my family: me, the matriarch; my sons, Chris and John; their wives, Sarah and Jen; and two children each, Henry 16, Phoebe 13, Sam 12, and Charlie 6. On paper we form a perfect triangle of a family tree.

A trip like this has been at the top of my life's "to-do" list for some time. Before I get too creaky to travel, which can come at you fast. Also, it's getting harder to corral everyone, with grandchildren growing up way too fast, busy, and heading in different directions. So this is the time.

I knew about these islands but wasn't sure where they were. "Where are the Azores?" people ask. "South America?" I didn't know that they are part of an archipelago consisting of 26 active volcanoes, eight of which are under water. I didn't know they are situated in the middle of the Atlantic Ocean, 850 miles off the coast of Portugal, the mother country. But I have friends who have sailed in these waters and have seen pictures. I was aware of their lush green hills and rocky coast, which as a tourist entices me as much as European cathedrals. The formation of the earth's crust has intrigued me since Geology 101 in college. Another feature: my daughter-in-law Jen's family emigrated from the Azorean island of Terceira to Rhode Island, where she was born. So I like to think I have a familial connection to the archipelago.

Although this vacation is my Christmas present to the family, I wanted my input to end there. First I'd tried to find resort accommodations through a travel agent, but nothing was available. The few choices were already booked. When I told the agent my son was researching Airbnb's, she audibly sighed over the phone.

Weary of making decisions on my own, I chose to sit back and let the others work out the travel plans. Let them research sites electronically for places to visit, car rentals, and GPS routes to get us about. I would fly with the Wakefield contingent (Jen and John and the younger grandchildren, Sam and Charlie) from Providence on the Azorean airline SATA, a direct flight into the city of Ponta Delgada. The Cranston Lees – Chris and his family – would travel separately, overnight from Boston.

Chris booked our lodging. Together we chose a townhouse-type residence on a narrow street, located in a compact little village ten minutes from the city of Ponta Delgada. Although I was not looking for a bargain, inventory was slim. No breakfast provided at our home but it was extremely reasonable. And with good reason: two bathrooms for nine of us. From my cruising experience, I knew about one "head" on a sailboat with seven people aboard. But we were kin. After all, the theme of this trip was family togetherness. A washing machine was included yet no dryer, only a clothesline. Those hardships aside, the view of the sea looked spectacular.

On Friday, August 24, 2018, we arrive in Ponta Delgada around 10:00 PM, local time, and take a terrifying fifteen-minute taxi ride to our home at Number 3 Traversa Madelena. With little traffic, the driver races at high speed, tailgating the few cars ahead of him. Maria, the home owner, stands like Juliet waiting for us on a second floor wrought iron balcony. The diminutive 40-ish Azorean woman, who went to U.C. Davis in California, is kind enough to meet us at this late hour. She walks us through the particulars of the house - little of which I remember the next day. She gives directions to a local restaurant, Cais 24, which stays open all night, as we are wilting with hunger.

After Maria leaves, we navigate the three floors of the narrow house and sort out room assignments. The ocean side is great, looking across a well-lit promenade with a lava rock formation over the sea wall. Not so great is the street side, especially with the high-pitched sounds of motor scooters, a standard form of island transportation. John and Jen get stuck with the "motor scooter suites," as the bedroom configuration worked best with younger children. No complaints from Henry and Phoebe on the hot top floor under a slanted roof. The two small bathrooms are identical, complete with bidets, and situated one floor above one another. The bidet, not being part of my culture, I use as a place to set my toiletries bag, for shelf space is limited.

We collect ourselves for the short walk along the waterfront (our stomachs are on Rhode Island time, four hours earlier). With refreshed energy Charlie and Sam run along the top of the sea wall. At the restaurant, which has the charm of a cafeteria, we order omelets and the comforting *canja*, a Portuguese-style chicken and rice soup. A darkly handsome waiter with high cheekbones and a ponytail, fluent in English, takes our orders. By now it's midnight; Cais 24 is doing a brisk business with the locals.

At 8:00 the next morning my cell phone rings from somewhere: under a pile of clothes. Surfacing from a jet-lagged sleep, I answer it. "Mom, we're on Traversa Madelena, not sure which house is ours." Chris and Sarah, Henry and Phoebe, had opted for the "red eye." They had landed in Ponta Delgada at 6:00 am, picked up their rental car, and had already toured the waterfront where the commercial fishing boats are docked. With the cellphone in the pocket of my bathrobe I go down a narrow flight of stairs to the street. There he is, halfway down the block leaning against a small red Volkswagen. With lots of waving back and forth he drives over to park in a space by the house.

"Hi Grandma," Henry and Phoebe say casually, piling out of the car hefting backpacks as though we were in Rhode Island. A hug from Phoebe and a partial one from Henry. These kids make my heart melt.

Soon everyone is up joining the arrival of the Boston group - some sitting around the ample dining room table, two lying in hammocks on the terrace, two flat out on the black leather living room sofas. Phoebe goes into detail about the man behind her on the plane throwing up. I love this, having everyone here, relaxed, laughing, talking. The only one absent is the original Charlie - husband, father, grandfather, who died in 2010. But "Dad" slips easily into the conversations, now and then, of stories past. I feel a certain weight in the air where he would fit. A grandfather who never knew his grandson Charlie. He relished these family gatherings.

Sarah, seemingly energized by lack of sleep on the plane, goes about making scrambled eggs. (Our host Maria thoughtfully left us a basic supply of groceries: eggs, milk, corn flakes). Three bags of Starbucks coffee I brought from home.

I'm very happy to have a real hot breakfast. Like hieroglyphics, the icons on the European appliances in the kitchen are difficult to decipher. Flames and bubbles and wavy lines. At first the stove is a puzzlement; eventually we figure out the nuances.

We are eager to explore the neighborhood and provision the house. Stepping out the front door, we walk in the direction of the swimming cove that Maria recommended. Traversa Madelena, a narrow street lacking sidewalks, has a European flair. Colorful stucco houses with solid wooden doors are joined side-by-side. In single file we form a line and head toward the water, pressing ourselves against a building when a car drives by. Except Charlie, who walks energetically in a jumping zigzag, heedless of the yelling adults.

The cove down the hill has a concrete pier with a ladder to the water, where a few local children swim. It is a cozy size with gouged-out places in the lava walls where ocean waves crash through. The kids brought masks and snorkels, and everyone swims and looks at marine life. "A lot of mullets," Sam reports. Charlie, with his olive-tan skin and swimming agility, blends in easily with the resident children. The skimpiness of Phoebe's pink bathing suit concerns me, but her taut body is beautiful, and tiny bikinis for 13-year-olds apparently is an accepted style by (reluctant) parents. I stay on the pier in my shorts and happily watch the good energy.

Regrouping, Sarah, Jen, and I walk in the opposite direction to the adequate market two blocks from the house. We are near the little village of São Roque which has a butcher, fish market, and apothecary, grouped around a cobblestone square. I bring my Stop & Shop bag, proud to have thought of such a detail. English is limited, but Jen's Portuguese kicks in. The grocery store carries everything we need for lunch: sliced bread and packages of ham and cheese. Wanting to buy a roll-on deodorant (I forgot to pack), I stand at a roll-on shoe polish shelf, unable to comprehend the labels. A table displaying a stack of milk in unrefrigerated boxes stands near the front of the store, dubious to me because I only trust milk chilled in a proper dairy case. But we know it's fresh. On future outings we'll see quantities of dairy cows grazing on bright green hillsides, the color rich as a well-fertilized lawn.

For dinner the nine of us walk 15 minutes to Mariposa, an elegant restaurant on the coast. We do not have a reservation, which concerns the Maître D, but he recovers and puts together two tables in a back room. I order an entrée of limpet - a type of mollusk that comes fragrant and sizzling in a square, cast iron frying pan. The presentation and garlicky butter are excellent. The limpets are not limp, but on the contrary, tough and hard to chew. The garlicky sauce I mop up with fresh Portuguese bread. Our waiter is dark and good-looking, with high cheekbones and a pony tail. He could be the brother of the waiter we had last night.

Trekking along the waterfront back to the house, Charlie and Sam climb over the sea wall and scurry on rough lava rocks. At our new home, tired at the end of the day, each person settles into a favorite spot to tap at their cell phones. Henry and Phoebe communicate with friends back home. Little stars of iPhone screens glow in the dark dining room, living room, and the two hammocks on the terrace. Charlie and Sam, side-by-side on the floor, backs to the wall, play a game that pings and whistles on their mother's iPad. In the living room is a TV with various components and remotes and wires that never gets used. After making a negative remark about everyone on their devices, I retire to my room and open up Scrabble on my iPad.

Most of us sleep erratically due to the time change. Sunday breakfast is leisurely; the shower routine for nine falls into place. One shower at a time with fifteen minutes spaced in-between for hot water recovery, reservations required. Mounted to the left of the kitchen sink is a gas hot water heater the size of a carry-on suitcase. Whenever a hot water tap is turned on, the gas whooshes into flame from a pilot light and the water heats. It does not take long to adapt to this spartan system.

Today we begin our explorations. The three primary sights I want to see are a dramatic waterfall, a thermal pool, and the legendary twin lagoons (called "Sete Cuidads"), reportedly one blue and one green.

First we plan to visit the lagoons formed in the middle of an ancient volcanic crater. With after-breakfast coffee, Chris and John work out the details and enter the destination in their GPSes, while I go on the terrace and look at the sea. Grandchildren run down to the cove for a swim, Henry and Phoebe in charge. The morning sun is full blast; bathing suits and beach towels clipped to the clothesline won't take long to dry. Not too far off, people are swimming with dolphins alongside a drifting power boat. A São Miguel tourist attraction. Not sure I'd feel comfortable treading water with those supposedly friendly mammals. But they do have sweet faces.

We start in tandem, two small cars, Grandma in the back seat of John's silver VW. Positioned between Charlie and Sam, I serve as a baffle in the event of squabbling, which can happen. Wherever I look, left or right, there are rolling hills and grazing cows, and the sea beyond. "How beautiful," "Wow," "Look at that," I remark at every turn. John drives, enjoying the novelty of a stick shift. Jen, with a cell phone in her hand, follows the blue "drop pin" on the GPS map designating our destination of the lakes. Somewhere we lose sight of Chris and Sarah; they might have gone on a different route. We take our exit at the confident instructions from the GPS announcer, the same woman who guides me in Rhode Island.

Driving along rural hills for several miles, we pass some houses. Then the geography flattens and we get to farms when the GPS lady firmly states, "You have reached your destination on the left."

The lagoons are nowhere in sight. There are some old barns and a farmer looking at us with curiosity. We try to call and text Chris; there are no cell signals in this location. I had hoped to buy a guidebook earlier but hadn't seen any stores, other than the grocery market. I miss paper maps.

By following road signs with little pictures of people swimming, we find one of the lakes. I'm not sure if we are at the green lake or the blue, but it looks blue. (The lore is: the green one reflects the hills; the blue one, the sky). There are lifeguards, kayak rentals, paddle boards. The boys swim a bit, change out of their wet bathing suits behind the open car door, then we drive up a steep incline to a panoramic viewing point. Charlie and Sam scramble up a precarious wall of solid rock while their parents holler at them to come down. John then scales a more precarious rock to take pictures of the coastline with his telescopic lens. Jen and I wander in the opposite direction to admire the hillside pasture. From atop a rustic stone, we burst into singing "The Sound of Music," expecting Julie Andrews to run up the slope at any moment. We do not see Chris and his family until we get back to the house later that afternoon. They'd arrived at the lake before us, did not swim, and continued on a separate excursion of their own.

With everyone weary, we eat dinner at home. From the nearby fish market, Chris and John bring back a local deep-sea snapper, which they prepare on a little charcoal grill on the terrace. Both in the seafood business, my sons visit fish markets the way other people visit art galleries. Even with a language barrier, they can speak the universal language of fish with the local mongers. Dining around a long teak table on the terra cotta terrace, white stucco house behind us, fish on the grill, we could be in a photograph for a travel magazine. Yellow and blue beach towels pinned on the clothesline add color.

Today, Monday, is the day for an excursion to a hot spring in a natural park. For this outing there has been a shift in passenger arrangement; Phoebe takes my place between Charlie and Sam, and I ride with Henry and his parents. Phoebe competently manages Charlie when he opens and closes his automatic window over and over. In our car, Henry sits in front navigating for his father. Evidently, due to a discrepancy in cellular data, the GPS gets us off on a wrong exit. Henry's wisdom and sense of direction take us back to the main route. (John has also gotten lost.) As we get closer to the hot springs, we see plumes of steam rise from a distant hill, and I am struck by the power of geothermal activity churning the depths of the volcano. The sky is bright blue with Cool Whip clouds.

The hot spring is not what I pictured. In my mind I saw a slightly gurgling pond set in a rustic cove of rocks. But instead it is on the grounds of "Terra Nostra," an art deco hotel that includes historic landscaped gardens on the site. We stroll through the misty woodland path that has a fantasy aura, only the mist turns to sprinkles, then all-out rain. We dash to the changing rooms, Henry the only one with a rain jacket. Holding tote bags on our heads, we join a short line of swimmers waiting for a changing room, and soon I am able to peel out of my wet clothes into a bathing suit. The concrete floor is cold and clammy from previous visitors.

The large, round pool is formally constructed, with mineral water cascading into it from decorative spouts around the rim. The only place we can store our belongings is under the slatted park benches, allowing rain to drizzle on them through the open spaces. Lowering myself down the swimming ladder, I push back and wallow in the yellowish therapeutic water. The warm and slimy sensation is like a bathtub filled with skin softener as it relaxes my body. A few smaller pools are on the grounds as well, left in their natural state. The volcanoes never rest.

Everyone refreshed, hungry, and back into wet clothes, we opt for the nearest place for lunch, the formal hotel. The manager graciously lets us eat in the hotel restaurant, even though we're getting the cushions wet. But of course he's happy to receive our Euros. Then we're off again in the car, our damp bodies steaming up the windows. Next on the itinerary is Nordeste, a town with an 1860's lighthouse at the bottom of another steep hill. That's what you get with volcanoes. The sun is now out, and a swim is planned in the lighthouse cove.

This is a seriously difficult descent. We park our cars at the top of the hill and walk down what seems like 32 stories. The grandchildren have no trouble getting down the narrow paved road on the volcanic slope. They reach a concrete pier as high as an Olympic diving board from which they fearlessly jump. Local children who live in a fishing village by the lighthouse are swimming as well. A few tourist-driven cars head down the road. We chose to respect the transmission on our rental vehicles. The crunch of grinding gears is painful to hear as they drive back up.

For this outing I only go halfway down the hill and sit on a stone wall while I watch the kids leap off the pier. My heart feels as though it might fall from my body on the ascent, and I have to stop every so often to catch my breath. I wanted to take a trip with my family before I get too creaky to travel, but I might have missed the deadline.

One night John and his family go into Ponta Delgada to visit Jen's aunt and uncle, whom she'd only met once in the U.S. way back. The uncle is a retired Supreme Court judge from Lisbon. Back at home they describe an American-looking house in town and an enjoyment of food and drink. (Drink especially, by the elders). Sam and Charlie, the progeny, are lavishly doted upon.

Our morning excursion is to Cha Gorreana, a tea plantation and processing factory, in production since 1883. It's situated on a hillside planted with rows of tea bushes resembling sculpted hedges. There's a hiking trail leading uphill as well. This is the first actual "attraction" we see with a gift shop, a cafe, and a sightseeing van of American tourists. So far we've heard very little English, only Portuguese, and have seen few tourists. Without a formal guide in the tea production building, we have to figure out on our own what this massive machinery from the 1950s is doing. Gathering, drying, whatever, and finally, six women at a table stuffing loose tea into single bags with their hands. The plantation's robust tea and fresh pound cake from the bakery is a restful highlight. And we start the trek uphill. On this hike we lose sight of Henry and Charlie. Having had enough, they opted to quit the excursion, and we find them in the parking lot getting to know a resident gray cat.

Our two cars drive to another natural swimming pool, a series of coves made from lava formations, down a steep incline. This is where I stay in the car and take a nap – not a light one, but the serious black-out kind. Later I discover my sons had researched online, "Where to swim in Sān Miguel." I think we covered all the options. I'm saving my energy for the waterfall (Salto do Cabrito).

Centered in the island's "most active geological fault," the waterfall is high and gushing and tranquil in a lavish forest setting. An abundance of ferns and bushes of wild yellow flowers and hydrangeas surround it. Again the climb. Some Americans in a four-wheel jeep pass us by as I concentrate on my footing on the pebbly, sandy road going down. There is always someone ahead of me, waiting for mom, waiting for grandma. I am touched by this, although I think I'm doing a pretty good job. At the base of the waterfall, Charlie and Sam leap deftly, rock to rock, in shallow water that deepens as they approach the falls. They swim, unable to touch bottom, in a spot gouged out by the cascading water. They swim behind the falls. Curious, I walk a bit, stepping gingerly over mossy rocks, not wanting to slip between them into the water, which I do. The flat space between rocks is sandy and shallow, although my shorts get wet. On dry ground, we are joined by the other family who had gone on a separate adventure, and we have a picnic of peanut butter sandwiches brought from home.

The final day before departure, I go into Ponta Delgada which feels about the size of Newport. Here I find a cathedral, plazas, and sidewalk cafes. The streets are lined with shops and restaurants, and no Starbucks. The pretty city is a refreshing shift from ascending and descending volcanoes. I go with John and his family, while Chris and his gang take off elsewhere. Jen and I are happy for the respite from nature and enjoy walking the pretty sidewalks which are inlaid with colorful mosaics. We stand in line to have lunch at Tasca, a rustic restaurant with a recent review in the *New York Times*. Impatient, Sam and Charlie chase each other around the sidewalk while we wait in the queue. I finally get to a bookstore with a shelf of guidebooks I peruse but do not buy. They feature historic villages, level walking tours, museums, art galleries, and maps. In hindsight, rather than take the passive stance at planning itineraries, I might have clicked on "things to do in Sao Miguel." At least for one day.

The morning of departure we clean the kitchen, make decisions on food: to throw out or not. A little of each. Maria comes to say goodbye and check the house, although she's pretending not to. John forgets his fishing rods packed in a travel case behind a door. That was the last he saw of them.

Flying home, I drift into a semi-doze, with images of lava coves and hillside pastures. Volcanoes, 500 years old. Many passengers on the plane are Portuguese-Americans, having spent summer vacation with relatives in Sao Miguel or Terceira. We fly over the Atlantic Ocean for four hours, seeing only water, until the eastern end of Nantucket comes into view. John points this out, he knows these things. I am happily weary.

*PS. In a January* New York Times *travel section, The Azores was ranked #9 of 52 interesting places to go in 2019. Two new hotels are being built on Saō Miguel. I am fearful a verdant pasture will be transformed into a golf course.*

# About the Author

Camilla Lee lives on the coast in Narragansett, Rhode Island with her cat and her dog.

49574390R10060

Made in the USA
Middletown, DE
24 June 2019